Sugar Skulls
Adult Coloring Book

By Shacream Artist

ISBN: 1530258987
ISBN-13: 978-1530258987

THIS BOOK BELONGS TO

_____

What Are Sugar Skulls

Sugar Skulls represents death, but in a positive manner. In Mexico it is believed that death is not the final stage in one's life but rather a step forward into a higher level of conscience. The idea of this tradition is that the Mexican families choose to celebrate the lives of their dearly departed friends and relatives as an opposite to how most American culture that tends to mourn the dead.

Day of the Dead (Dia de los Muertos) is a holiday celebrated in Mexico November 1st and 2nd. It is believed that the gates of heaven are opened at 12am October 31 and smaller skulls are placed on the offrenda (altar) on November 1st, representing the children who have passed away. Larger, more detailed ones would then replace them on the 2nd November, which represent the adults. The departed are believed to return home to enjoy the offerings on the altar. On that evening of November 2nd the festivities are then moved to the cemetery. People play games, listen to music, and place sugar skulls with the loved one name on the head of skull on the tomb.

Sugar skulls are often used to decorate the gravestones of the deceased. The reason they are called "sugar skulls" is because the authentic sugar skulls were made out of clay molded sugar, decorated with feathers, colored beads, foils and icing. These sugar skulls are very colorful and whimsical, not scary at all. Marigolds are also placed around skulls (marigold is perceived as the flower of the dead), candles and maybe even the deceased's favorite food and beverage in order to encourage and guide him back to earth.

Supposedly the symbolism of a sugar skull is rooted in the decoration around the eyes. Flowers are meant to symbolize life, while cob webs symbolize death. Burning candles set inside the eyes are a sign of remembrance. These items can also be used in combination to personalize the main focus of the skull as well.

Whilst the tradition of making skulls from sugar is certainly Mexican, the idea to use sugar as decoration in the first place came to Mexico from Italy. The Italians used sugar to make decorations during Easter, such as sugar lambs and angels. Therefore, when Italian missionaries came to Mexico they taught Mexicans who were cash poor but sugar rich to make decorations for the church in this way.

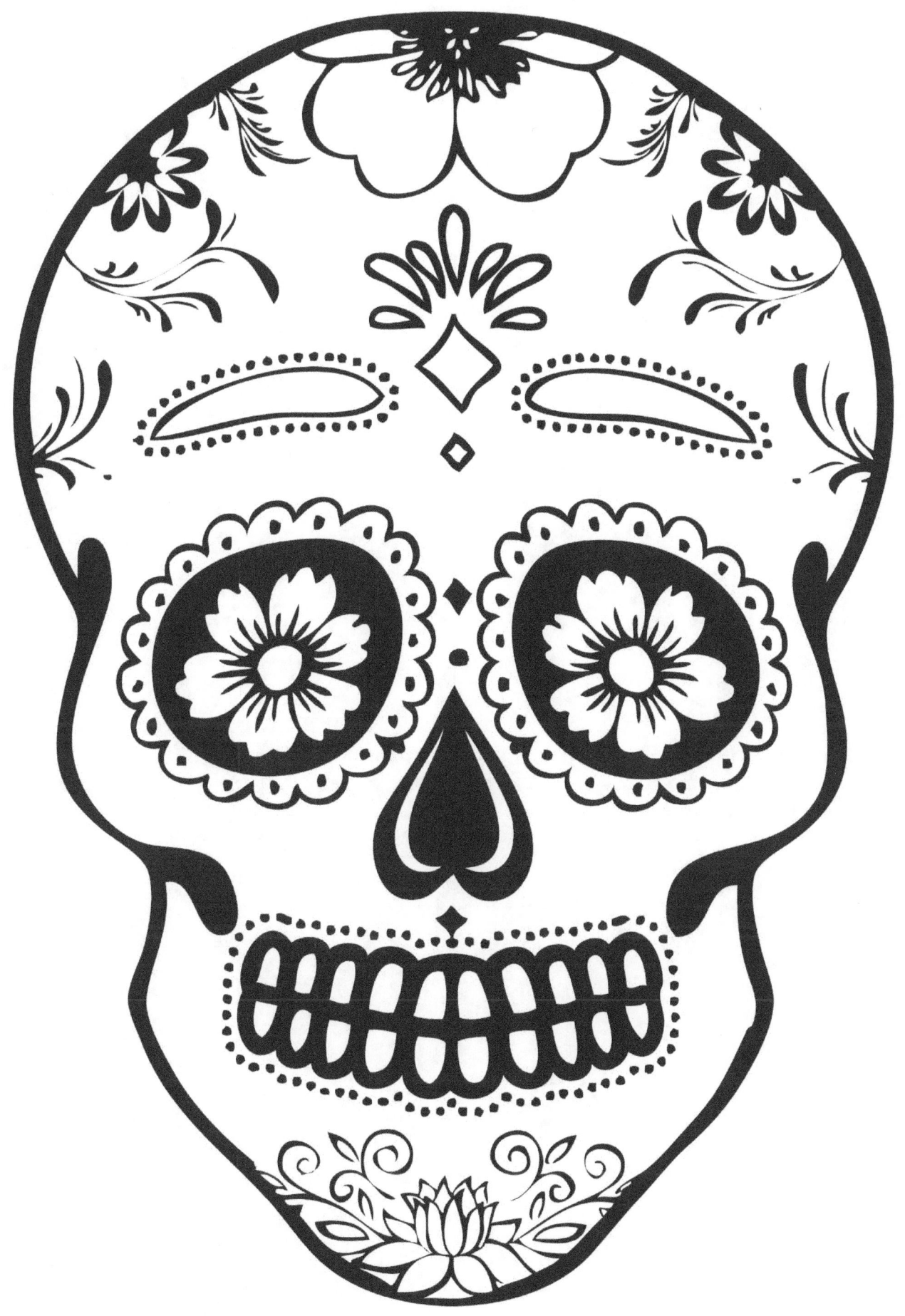

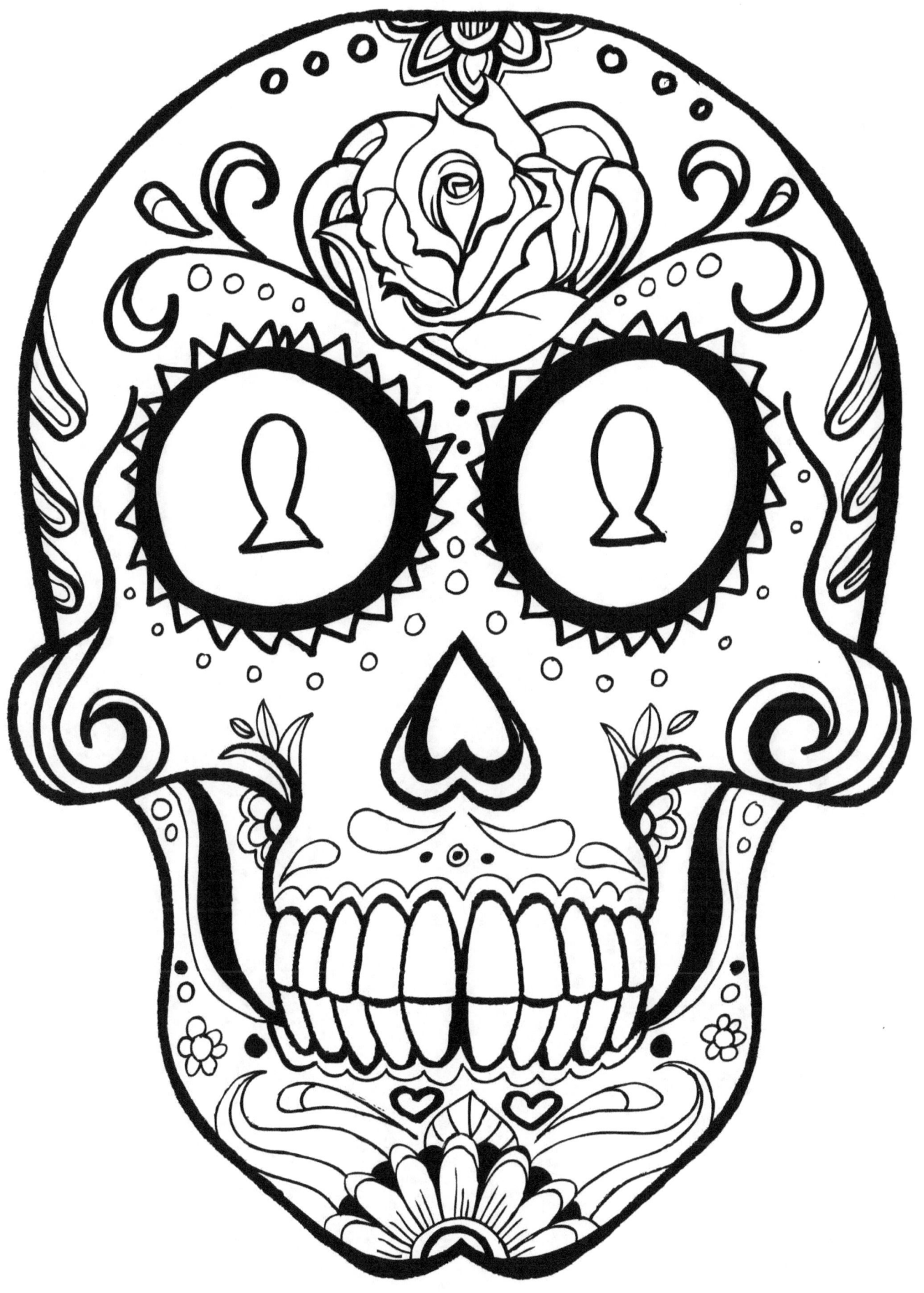

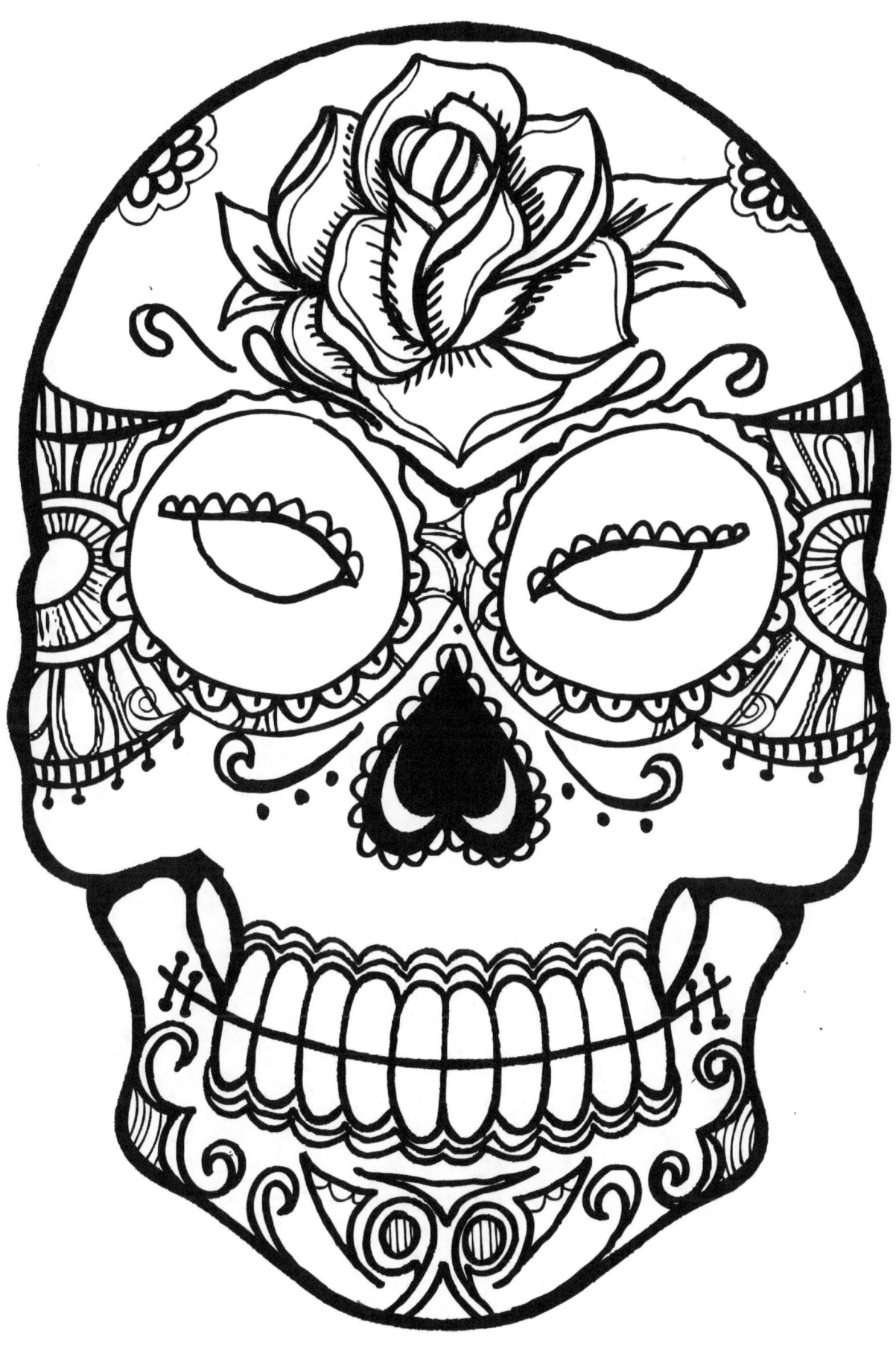

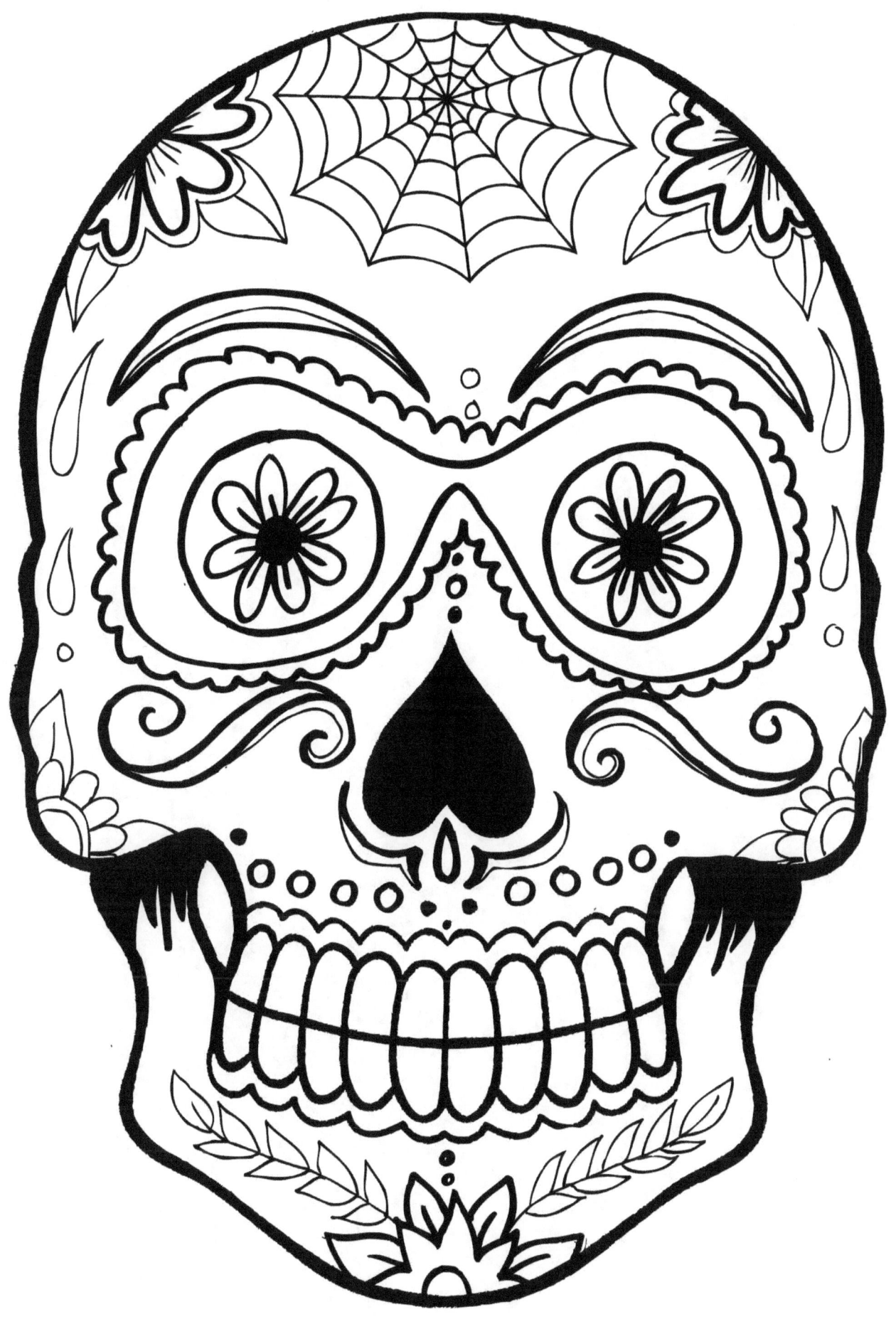

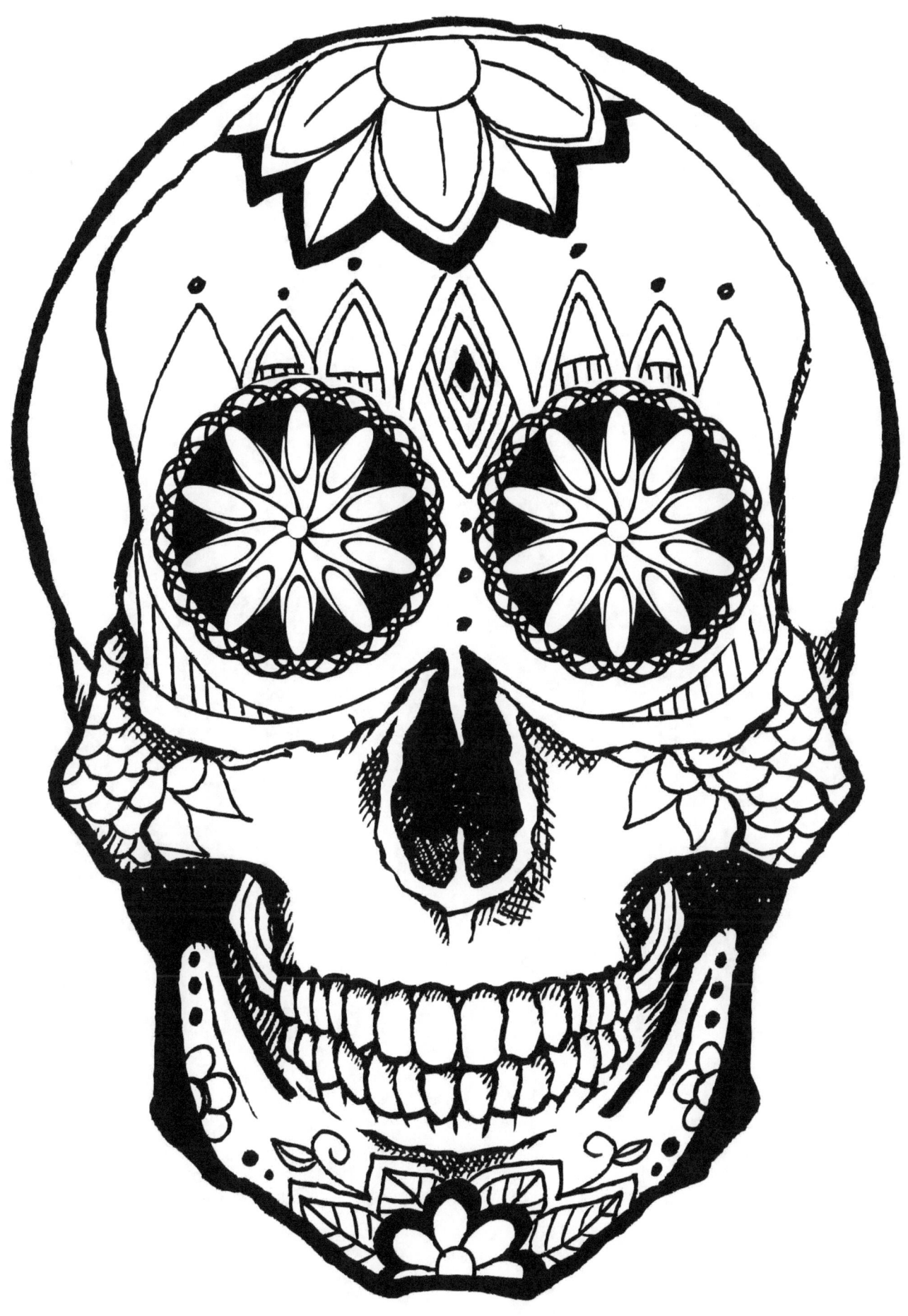

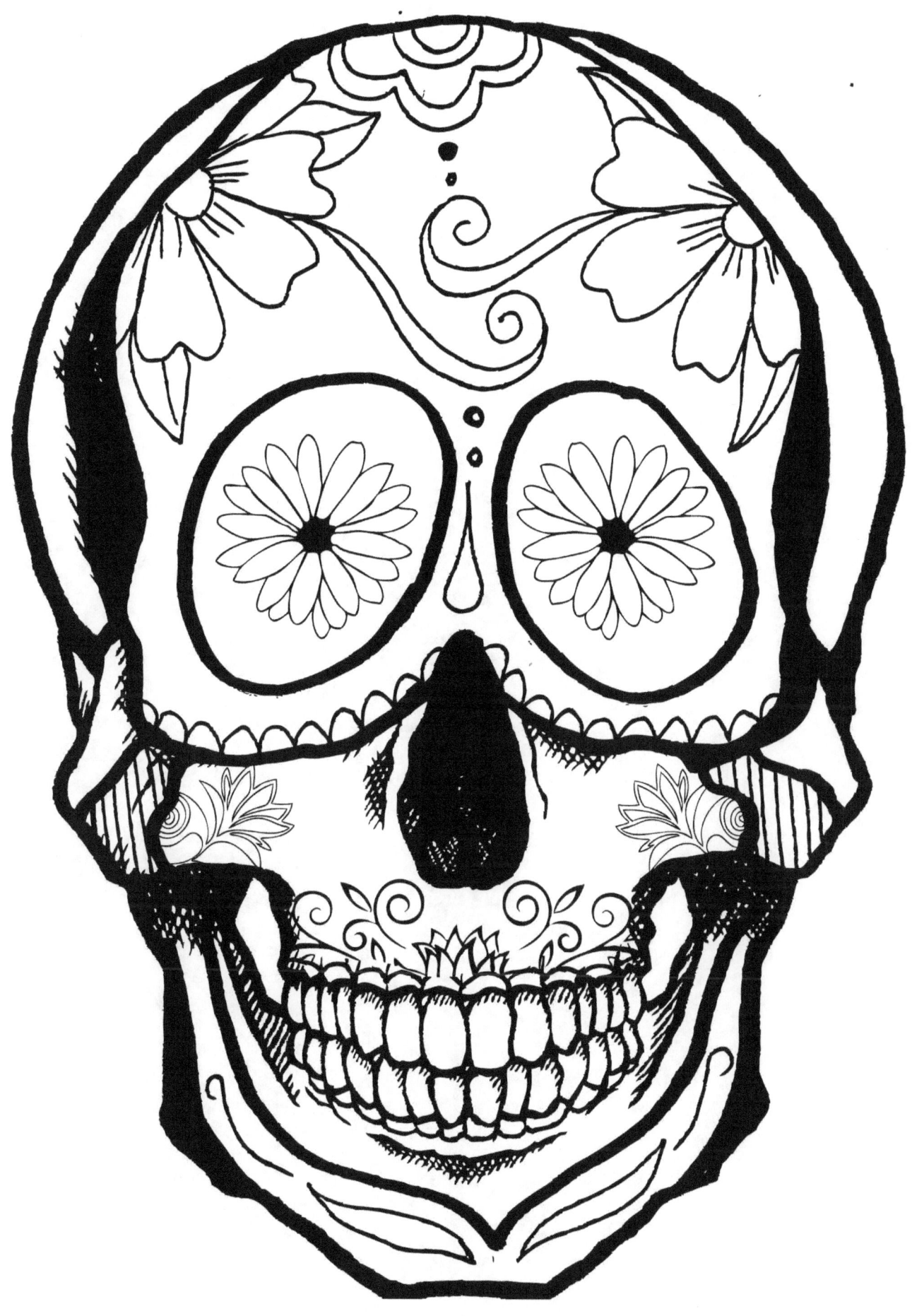

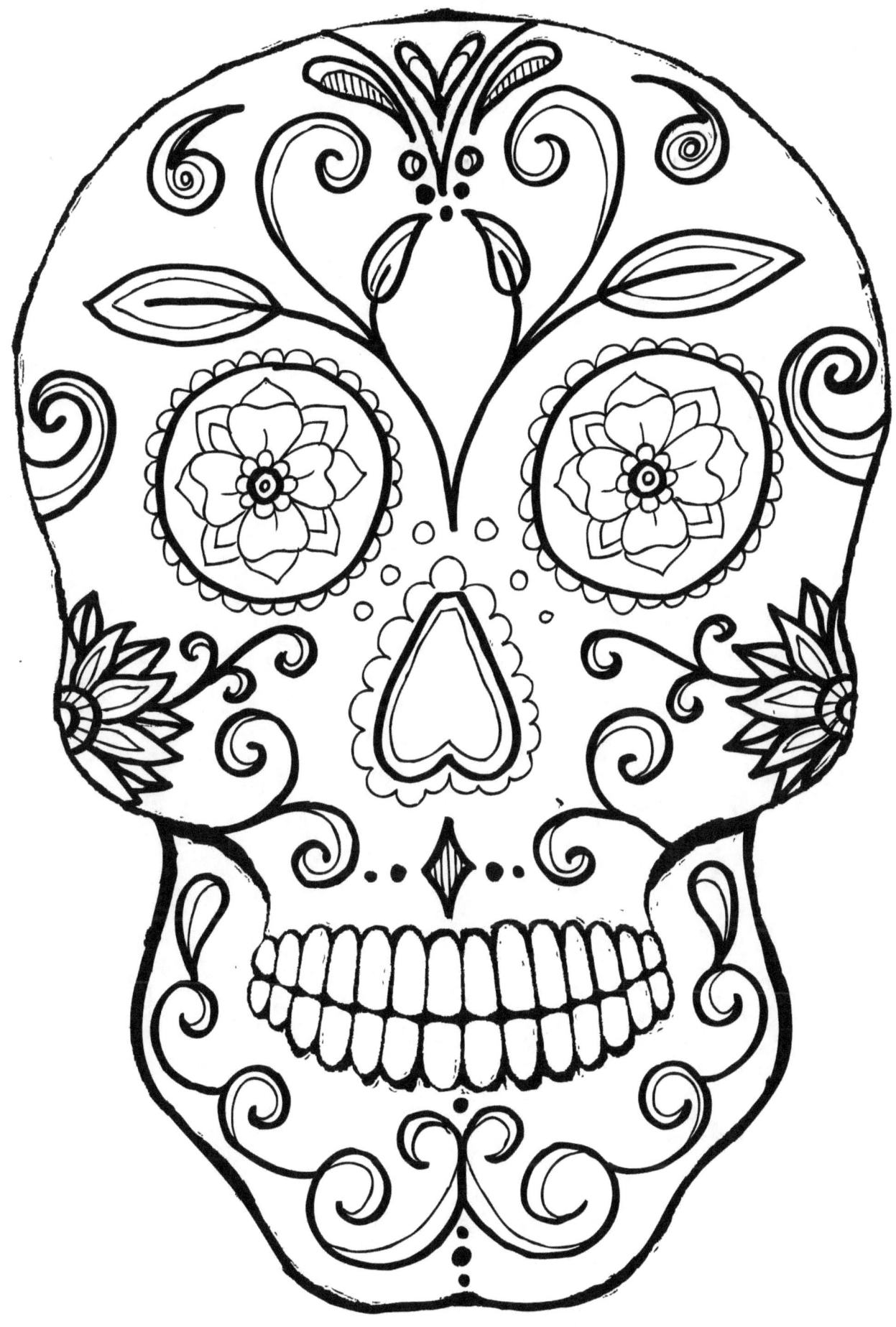

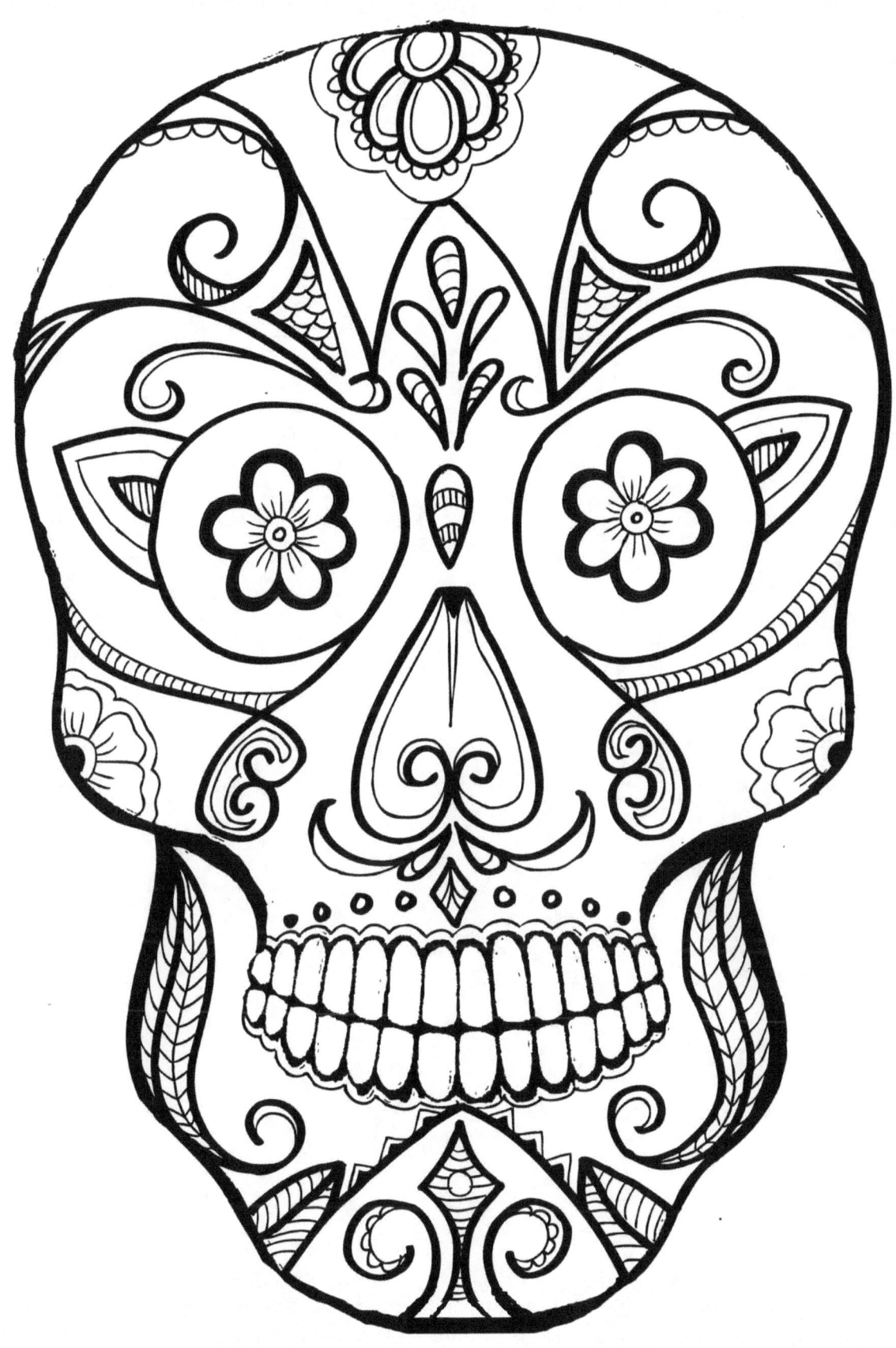

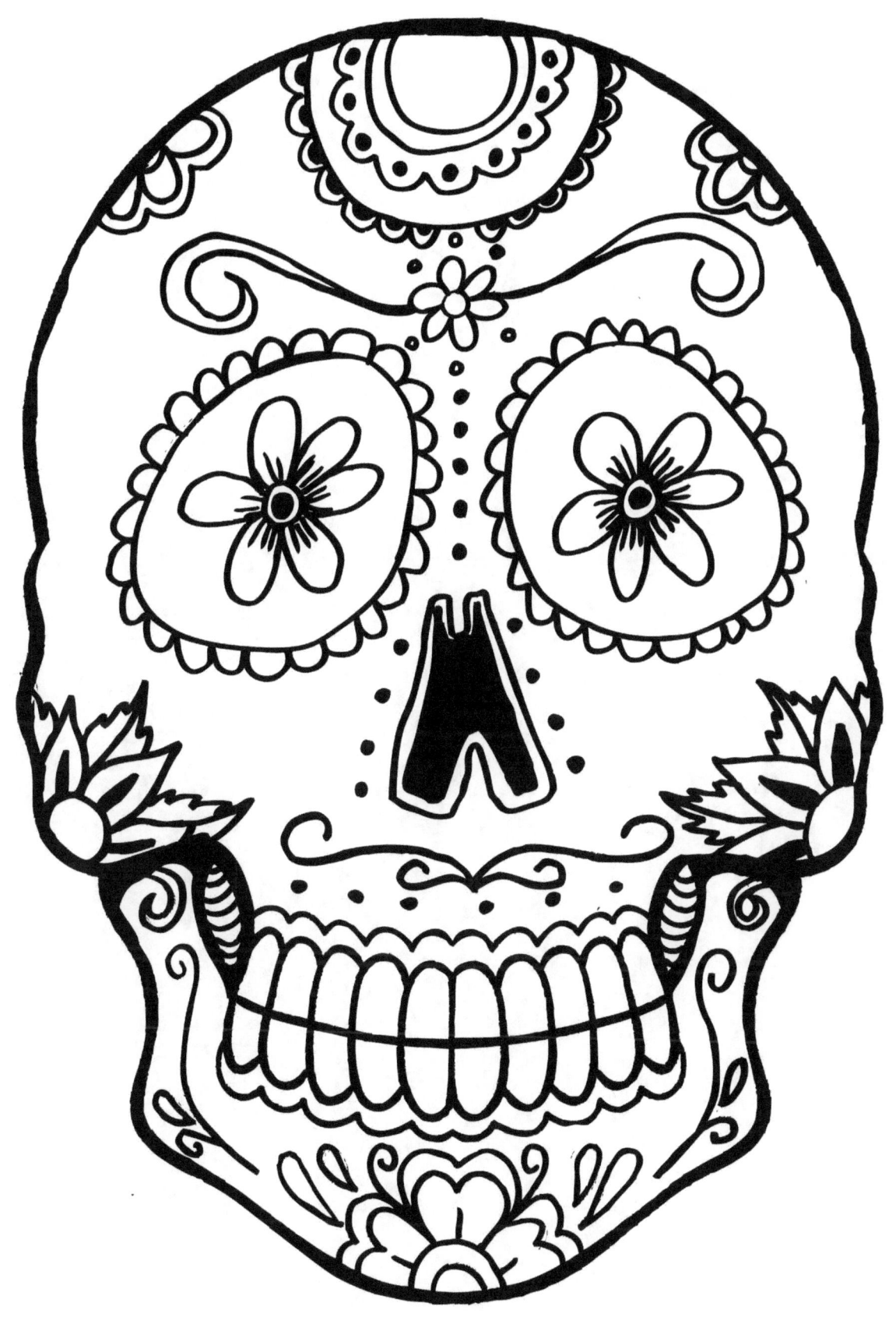

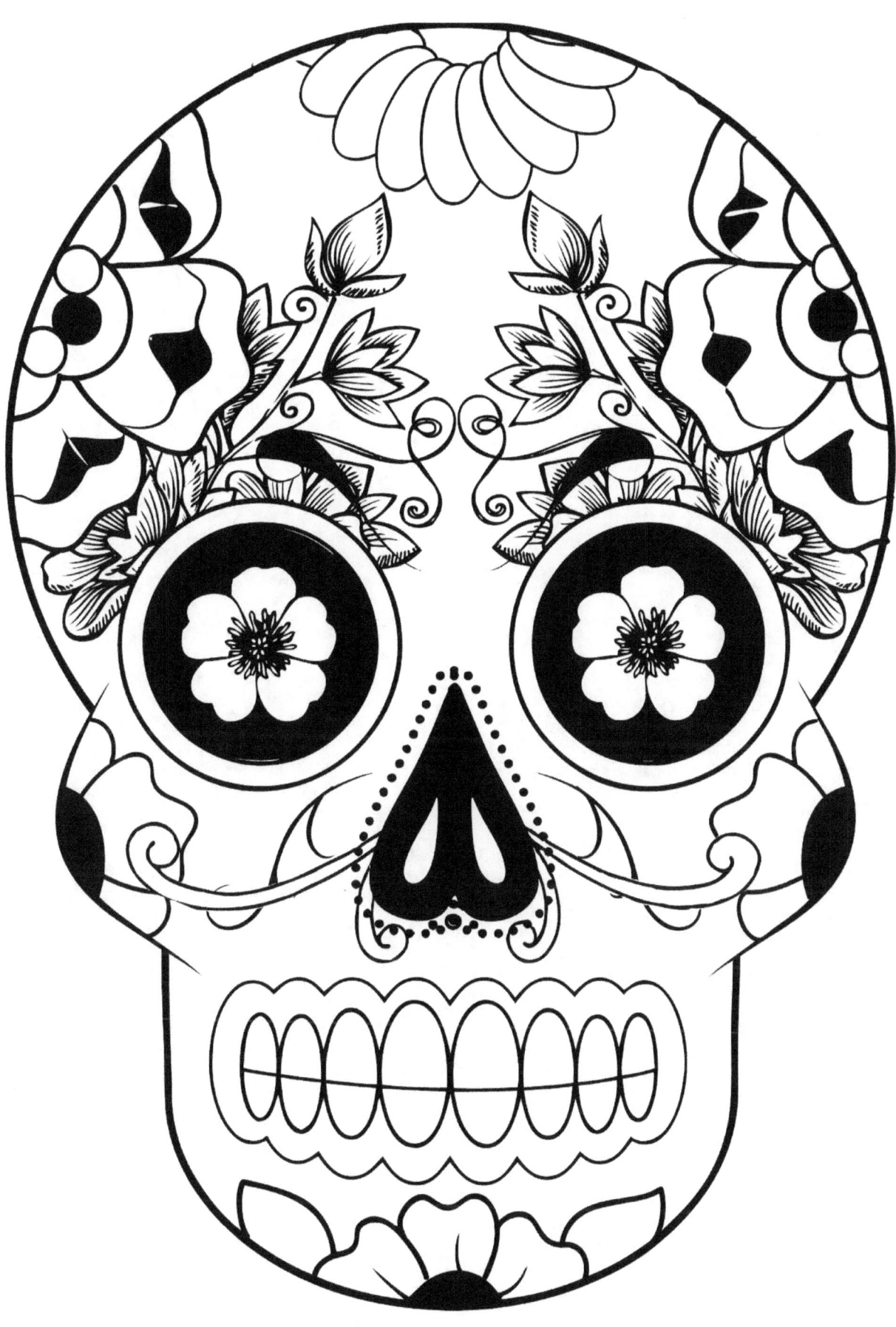

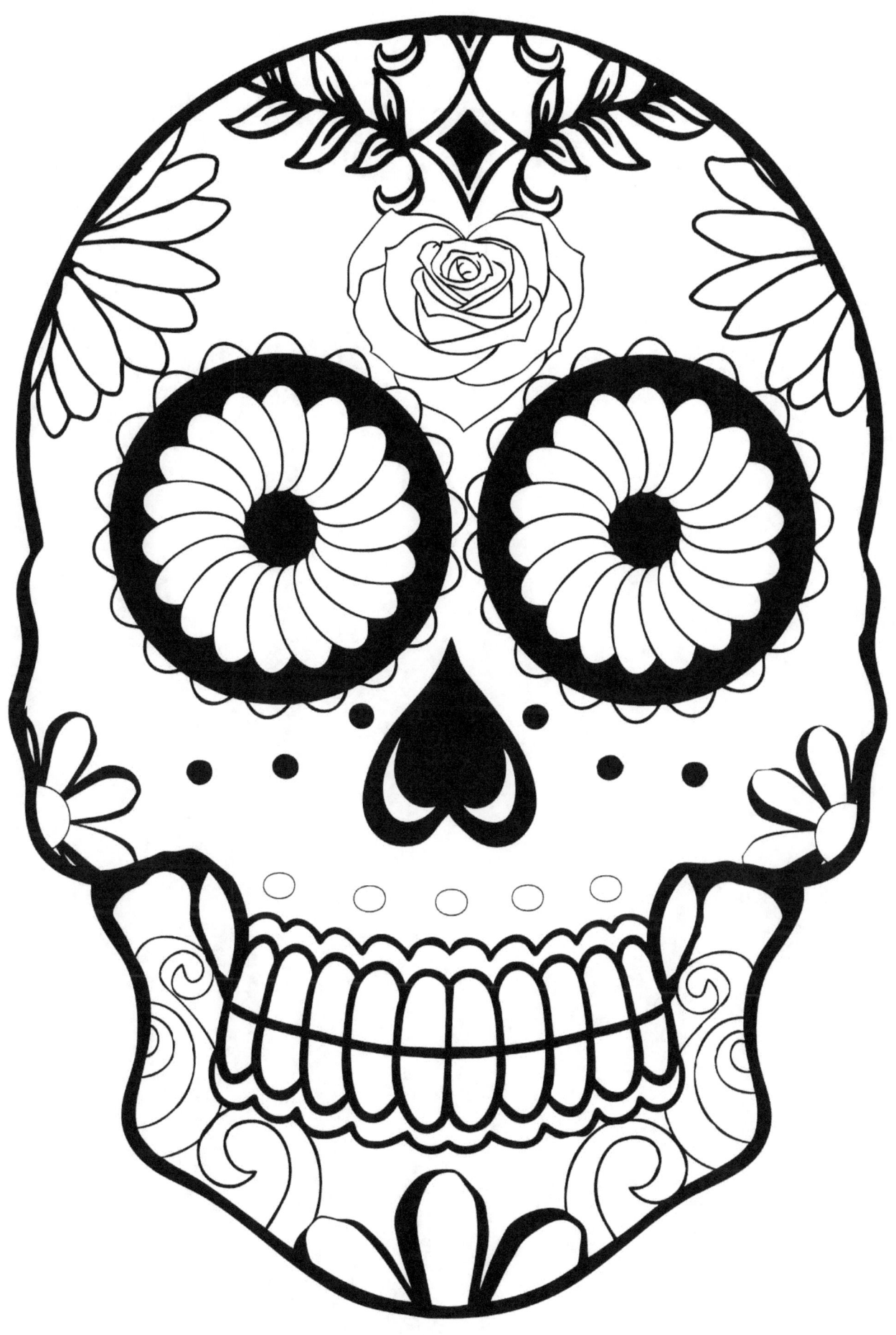

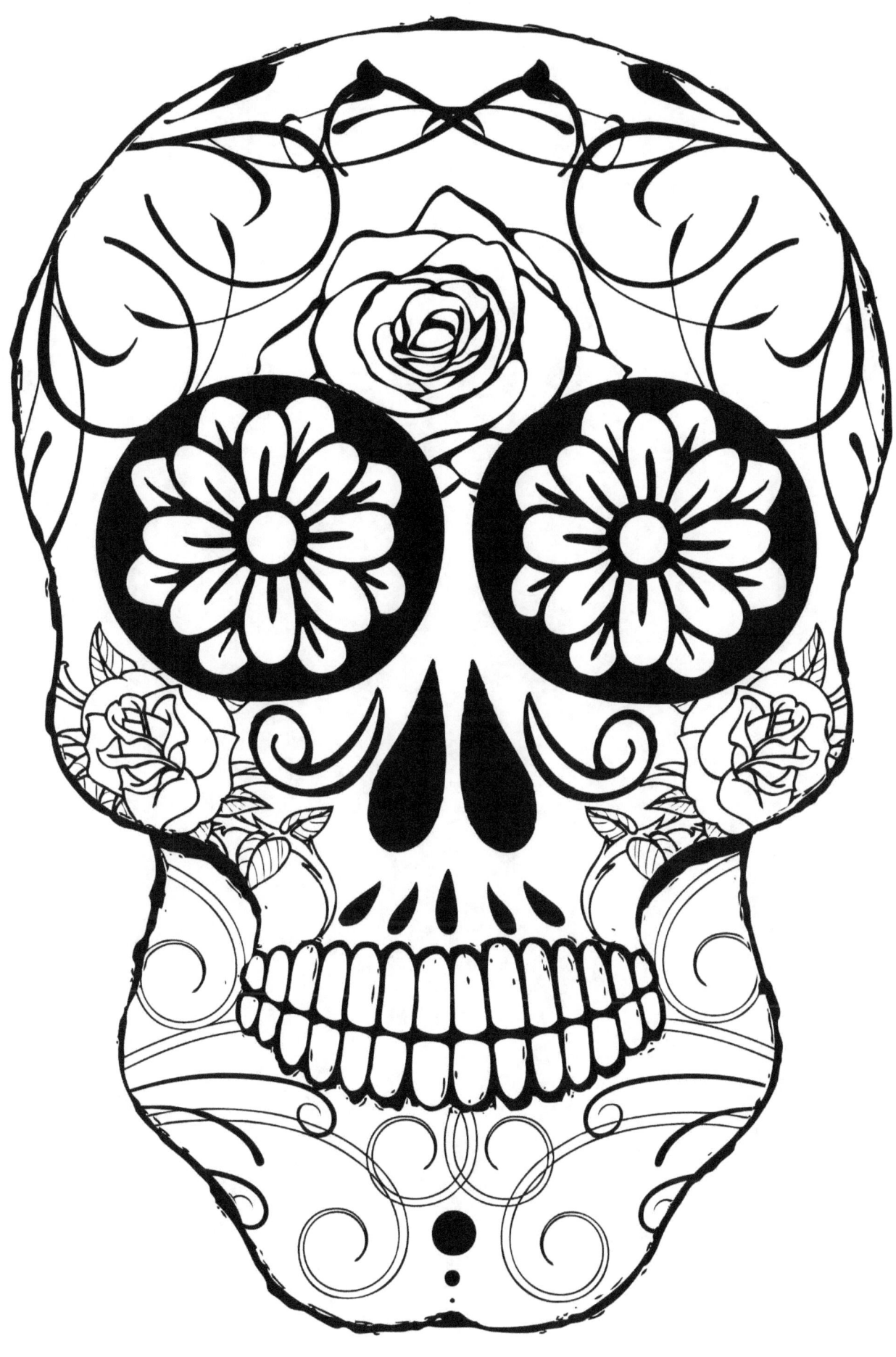

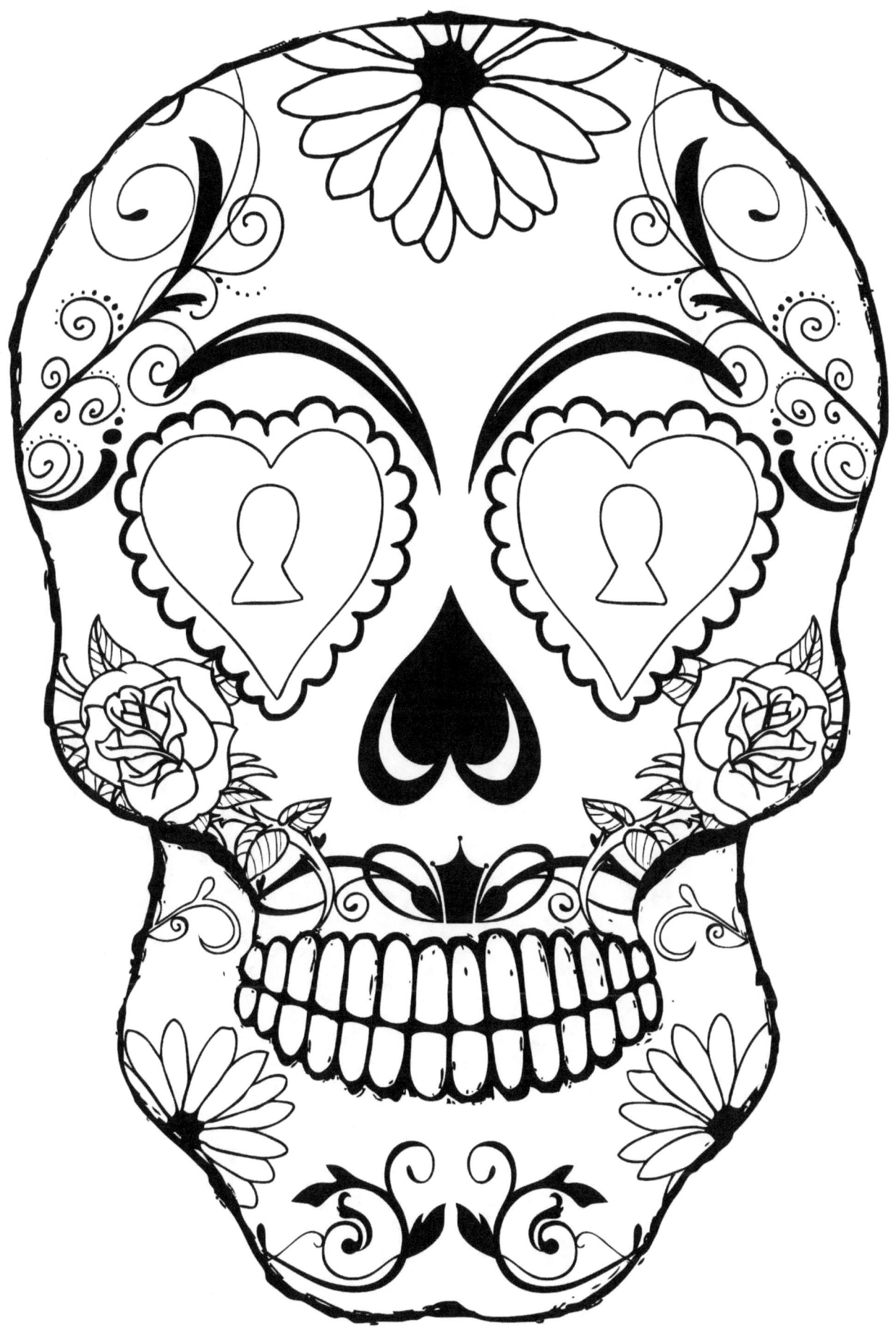

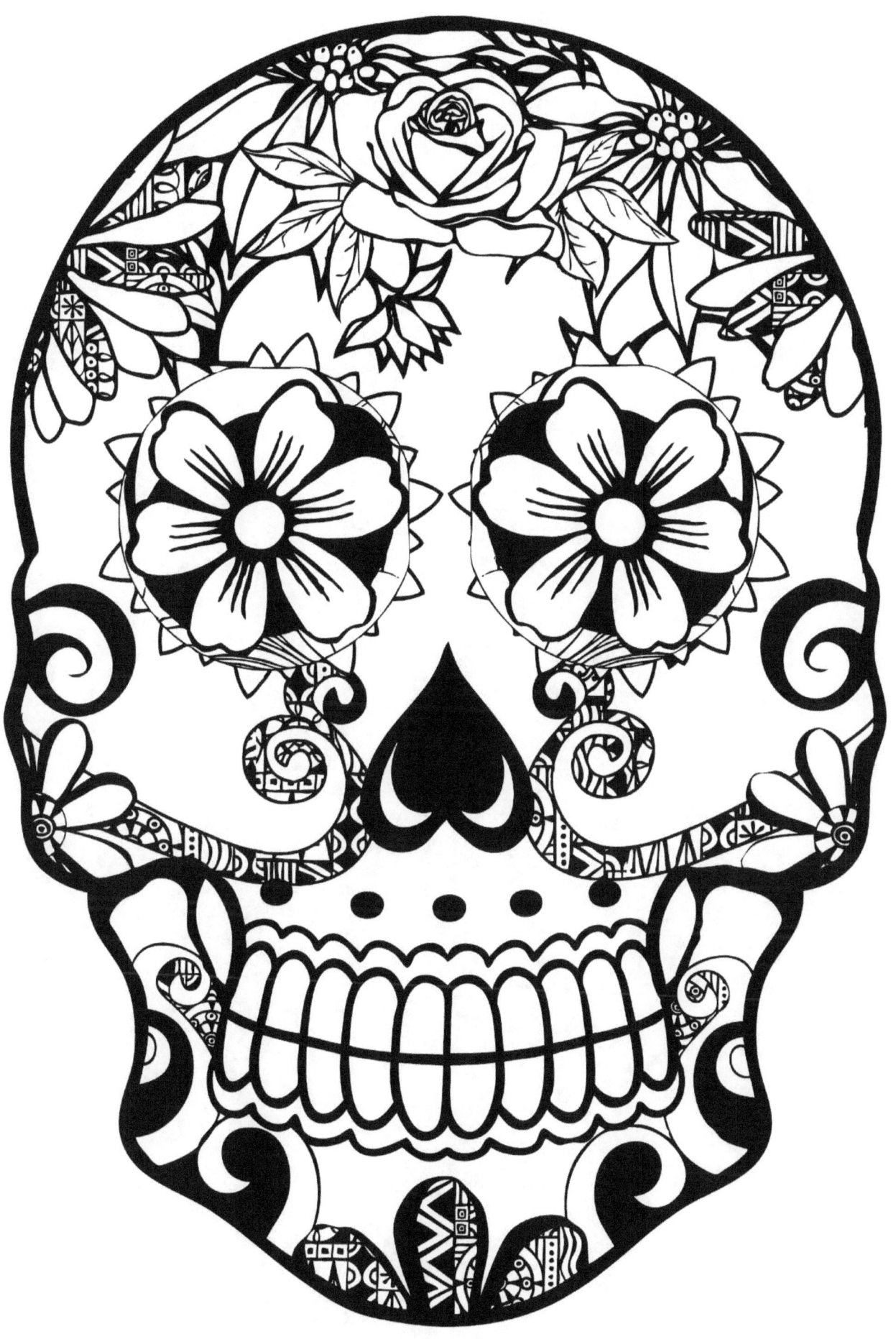

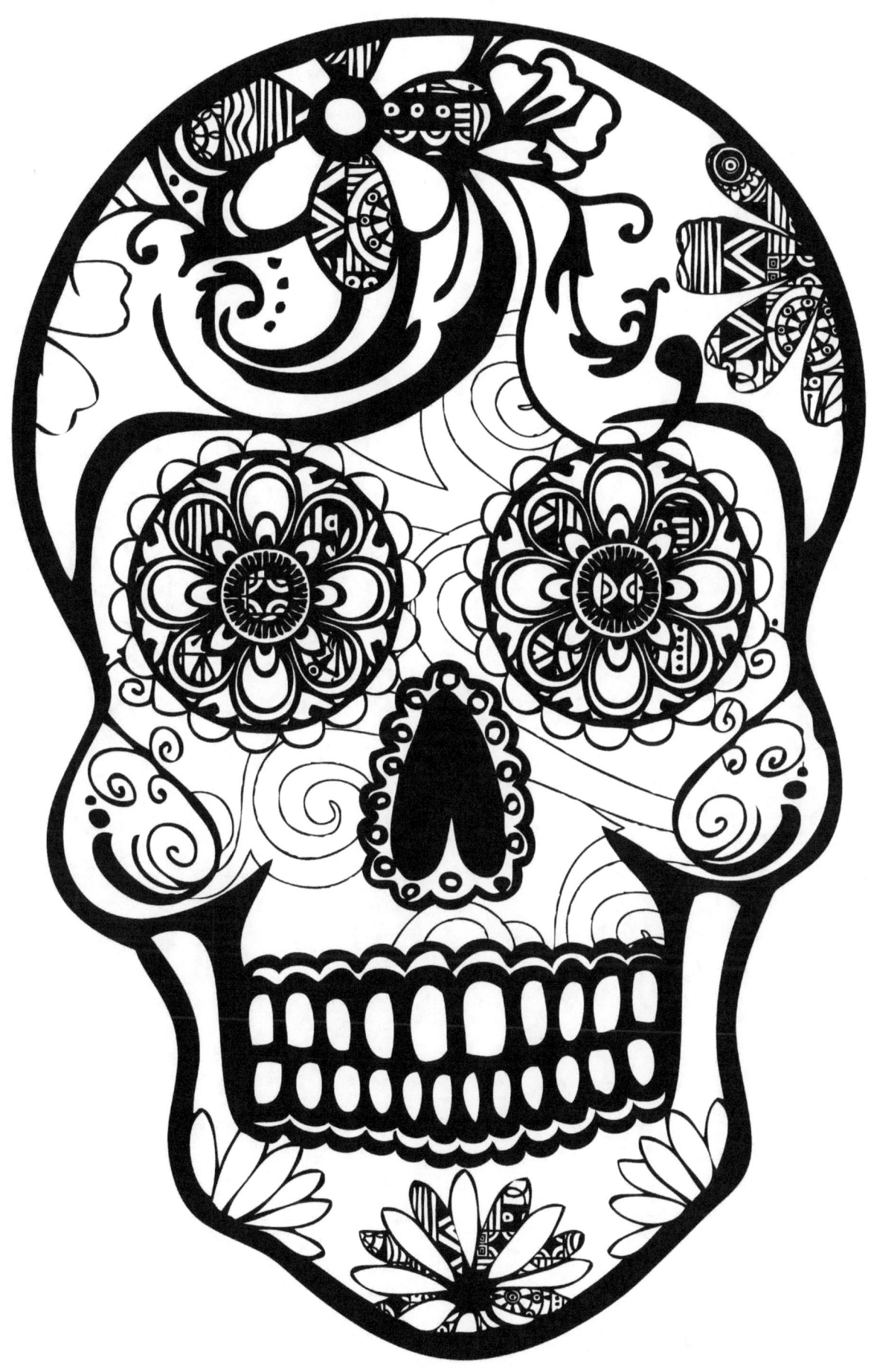

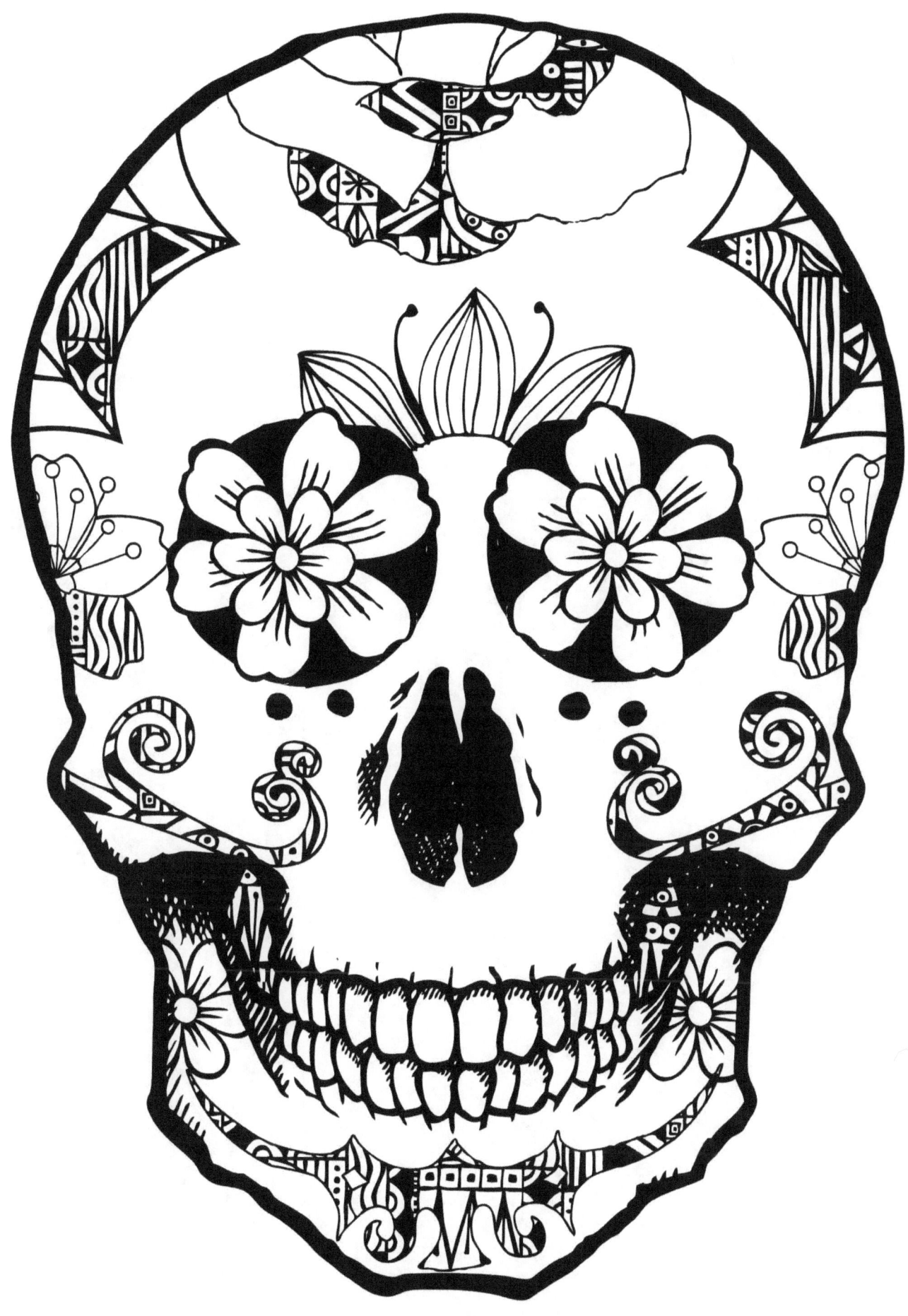

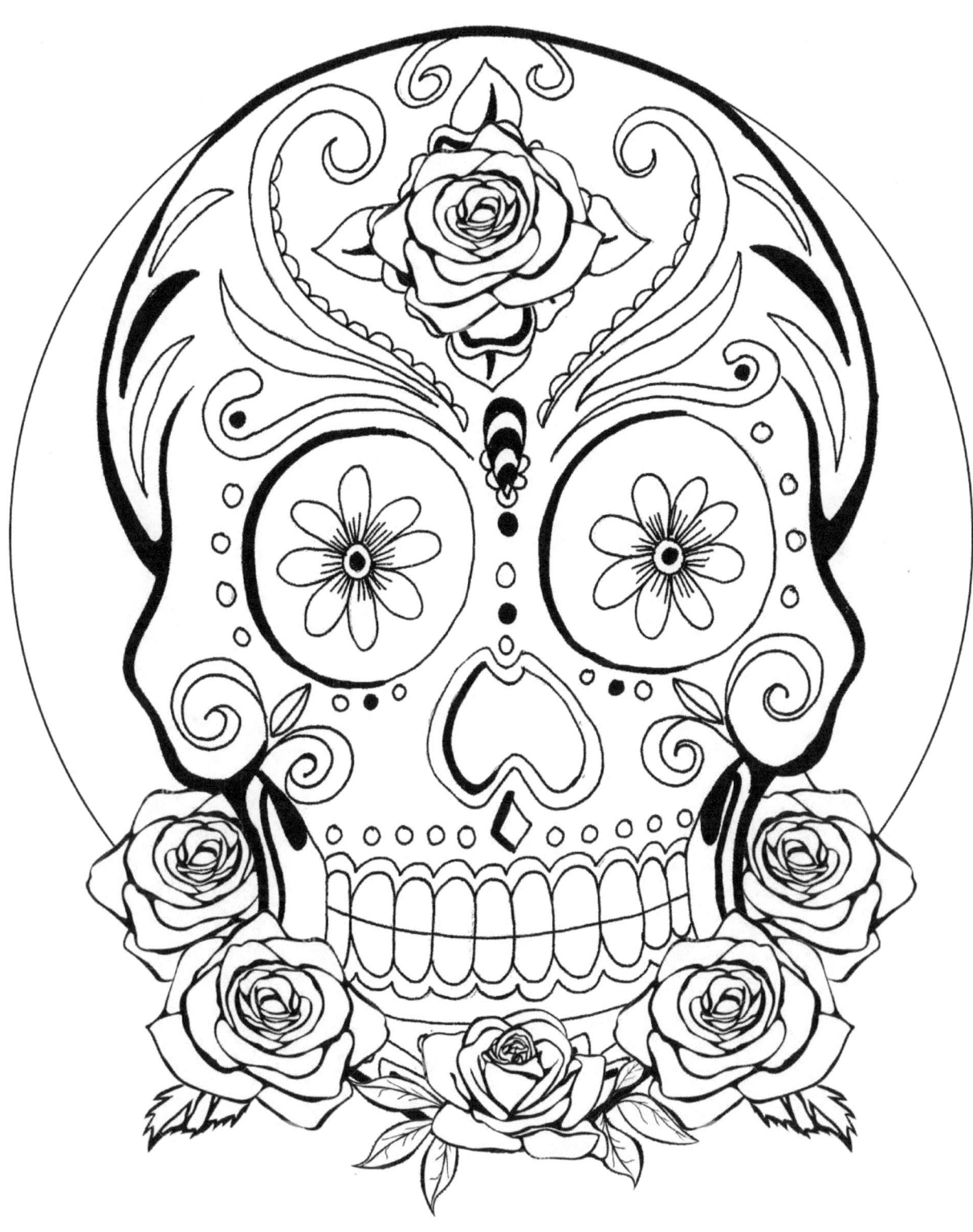

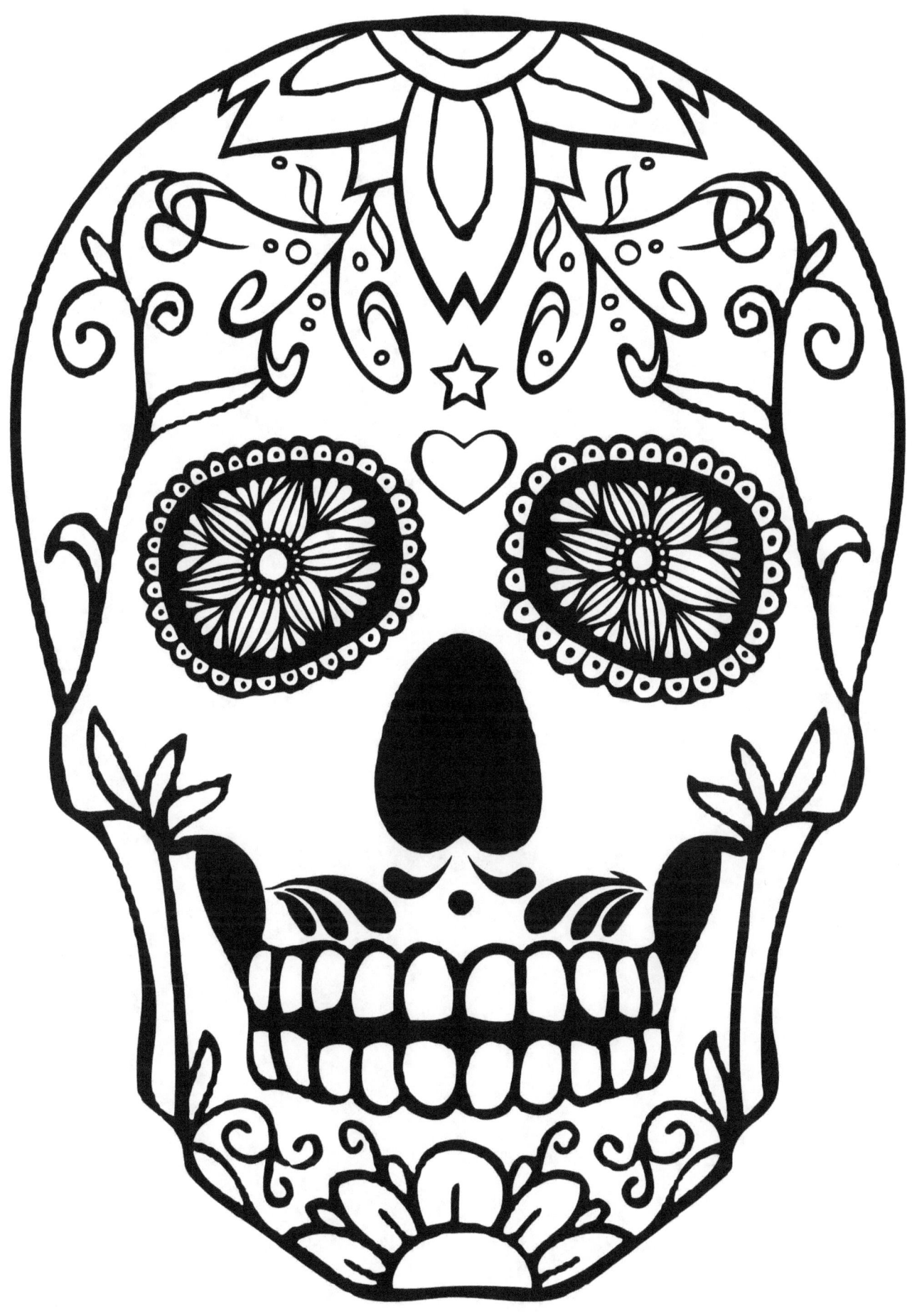

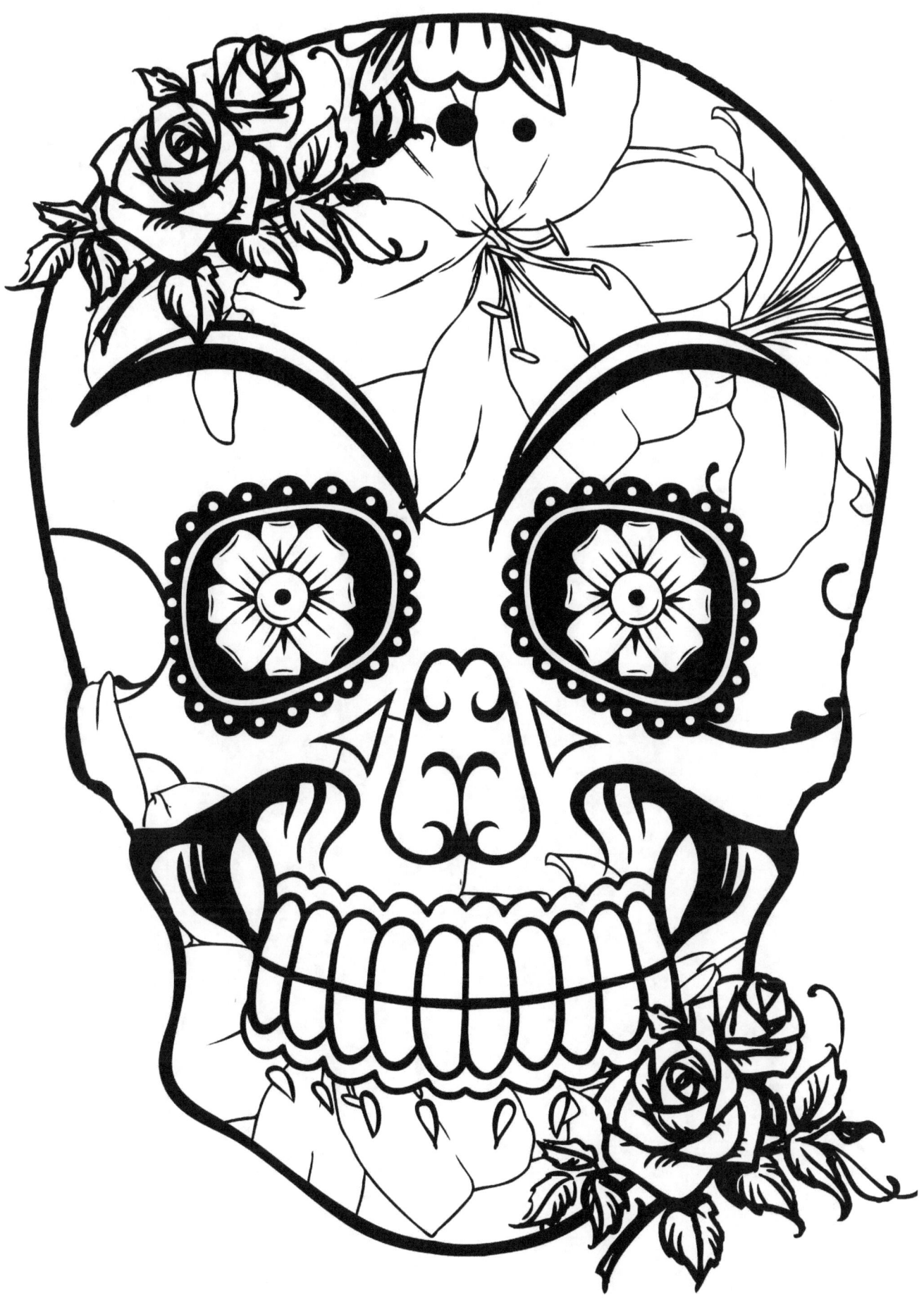

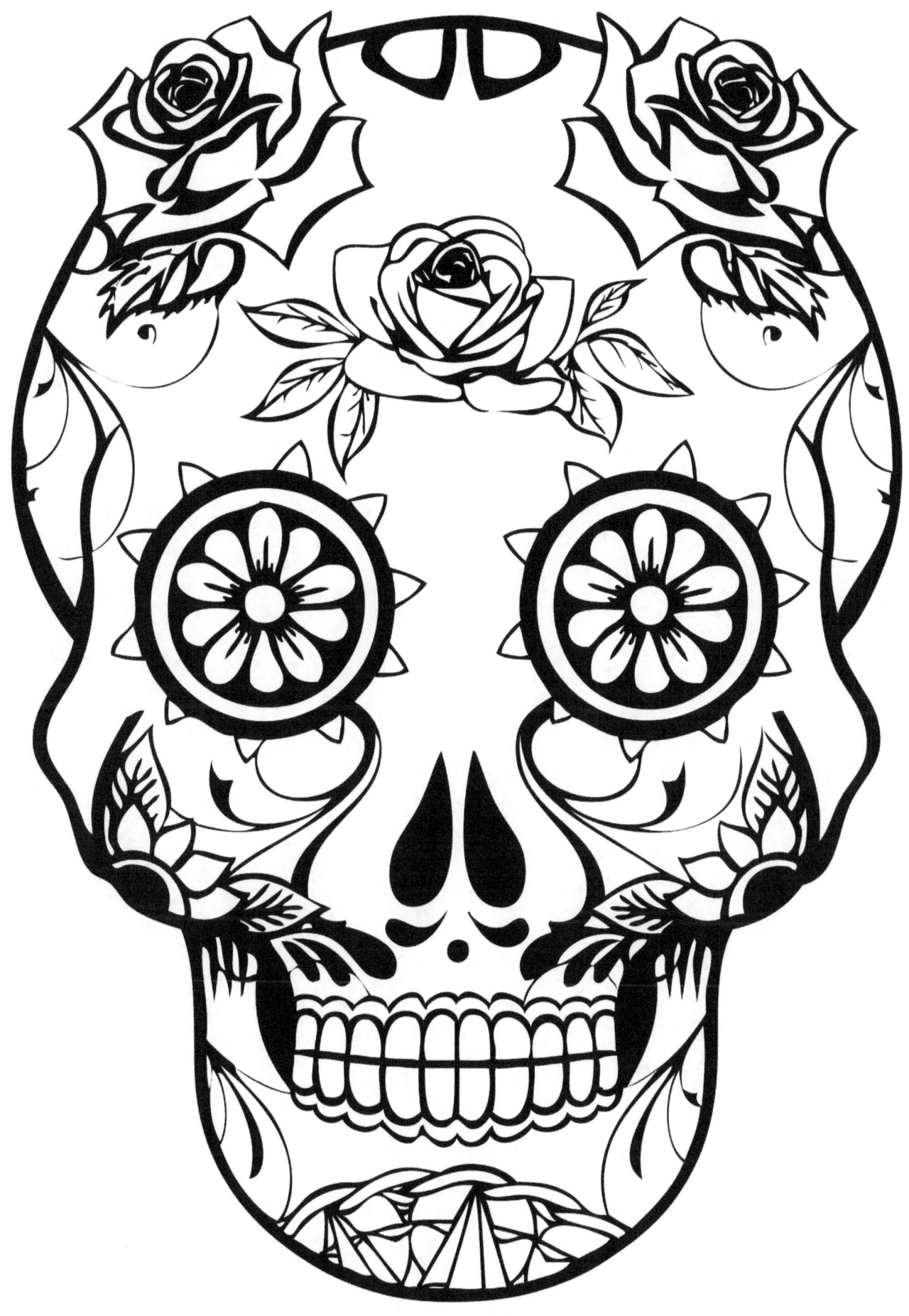

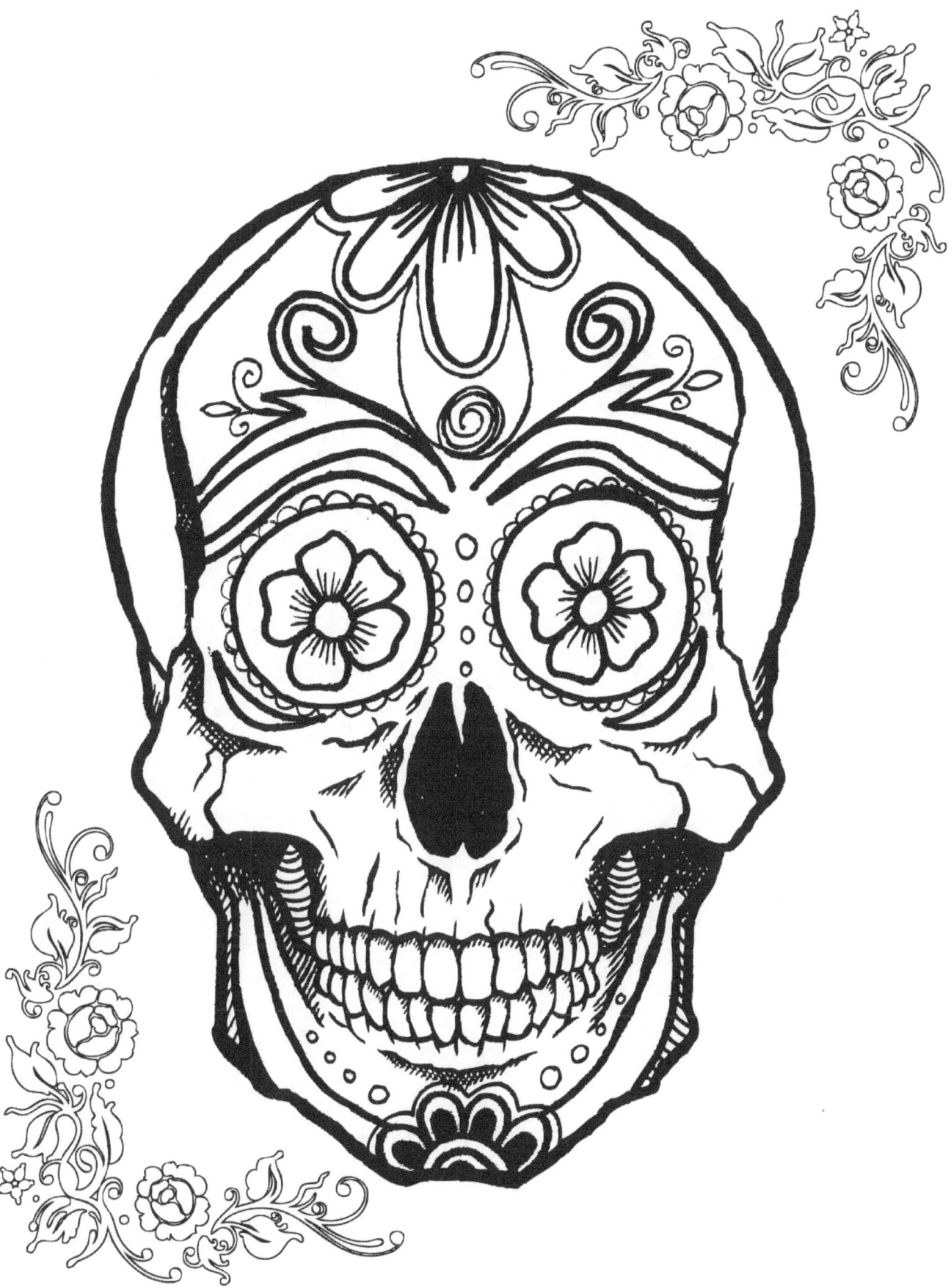

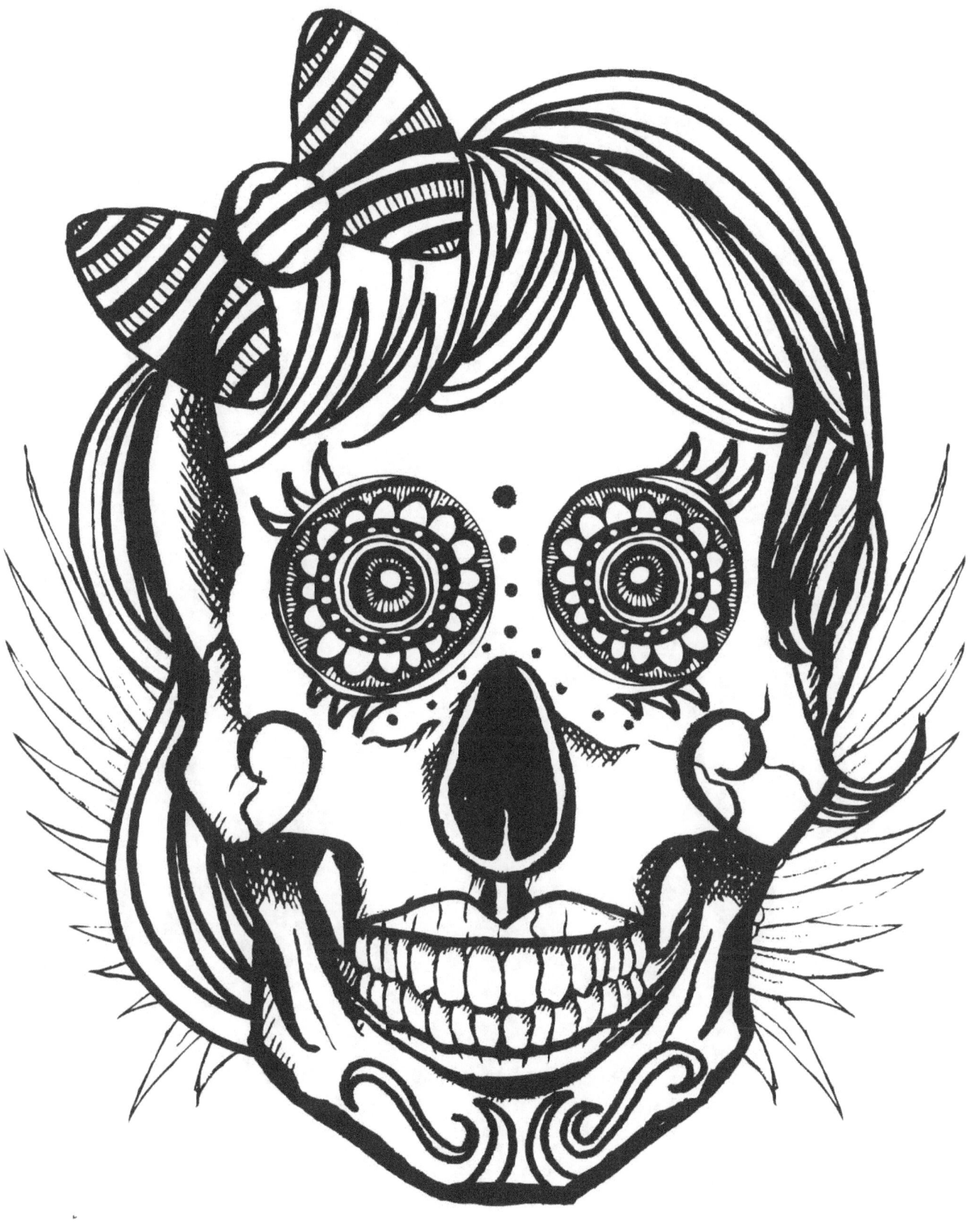

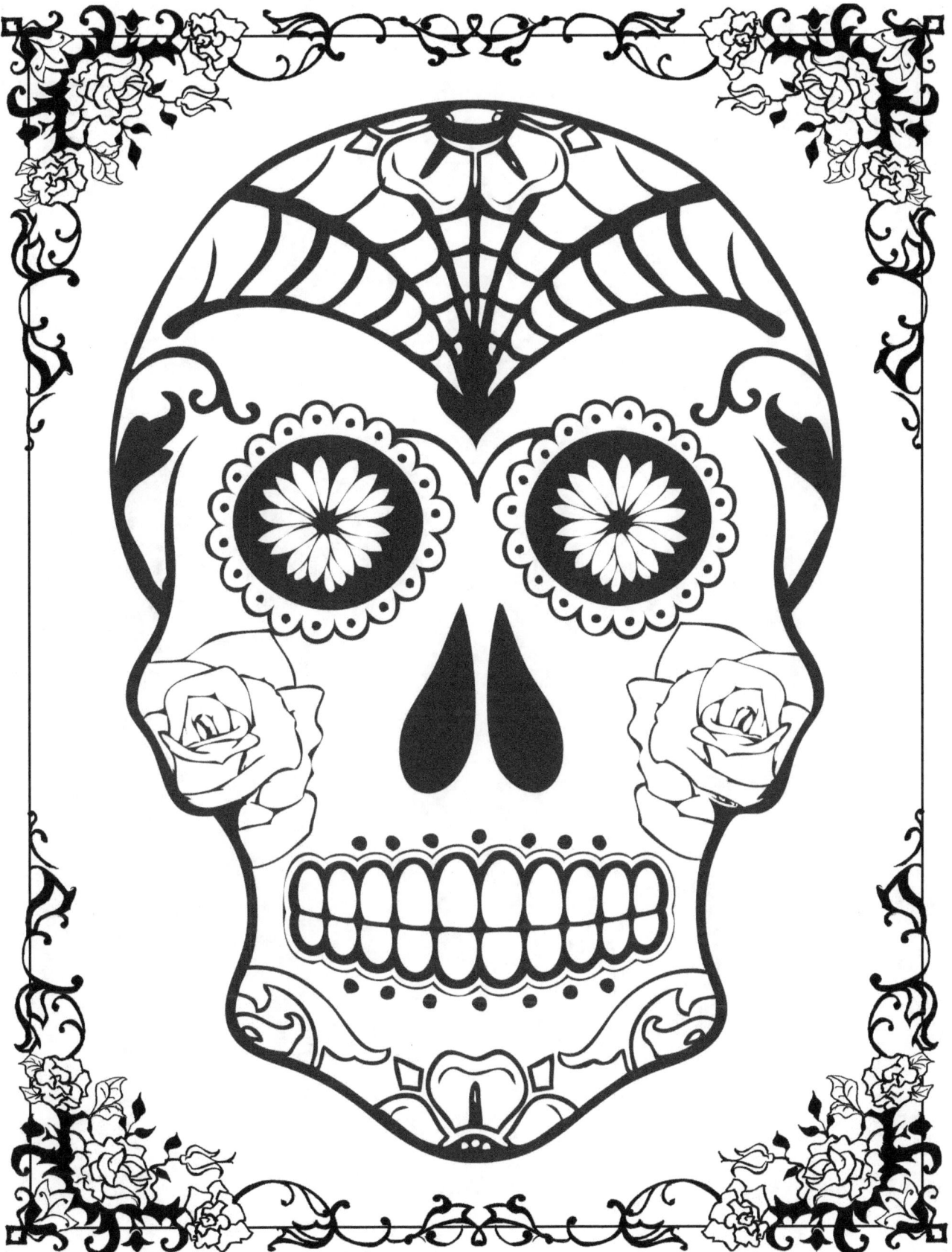

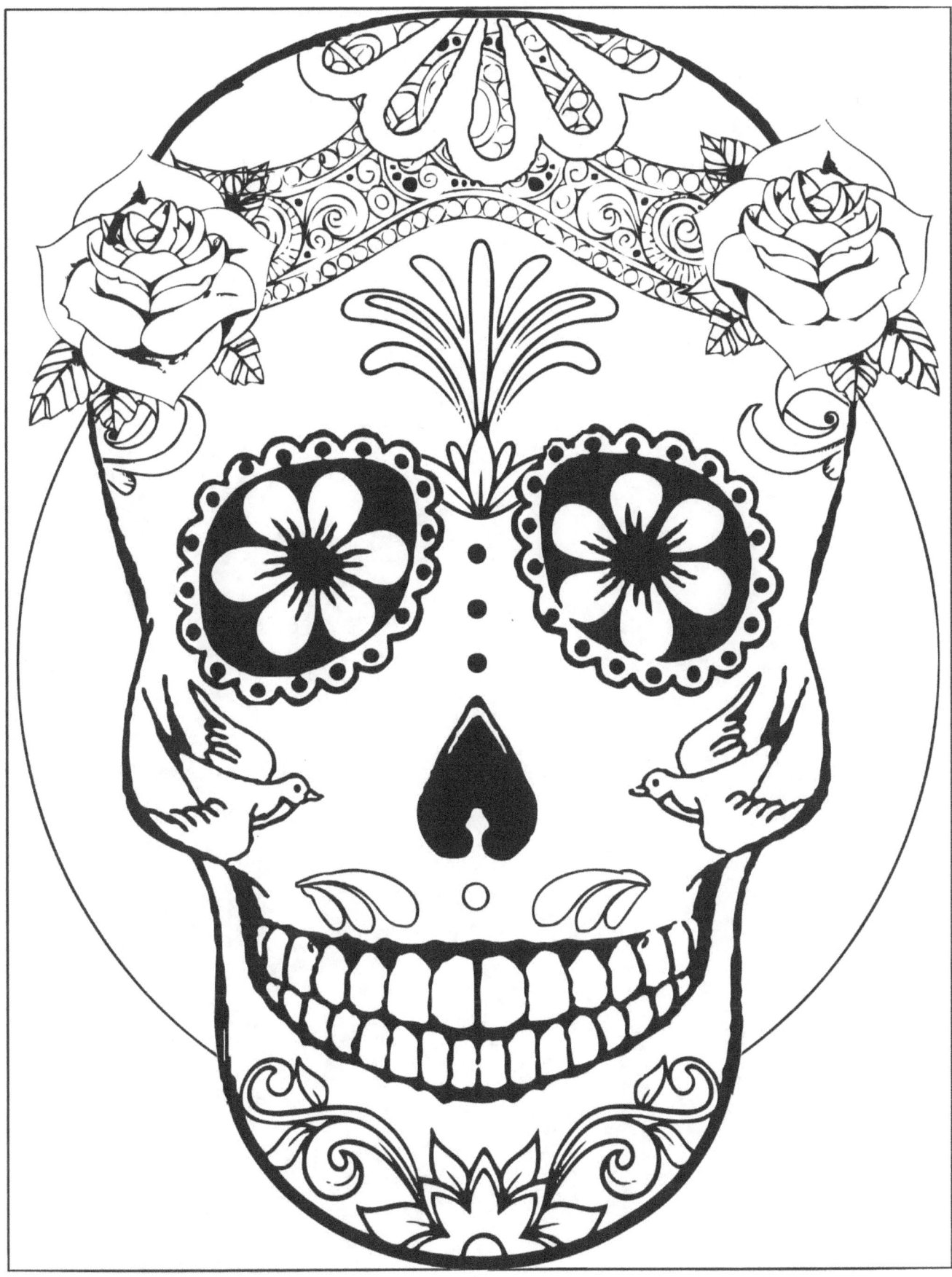

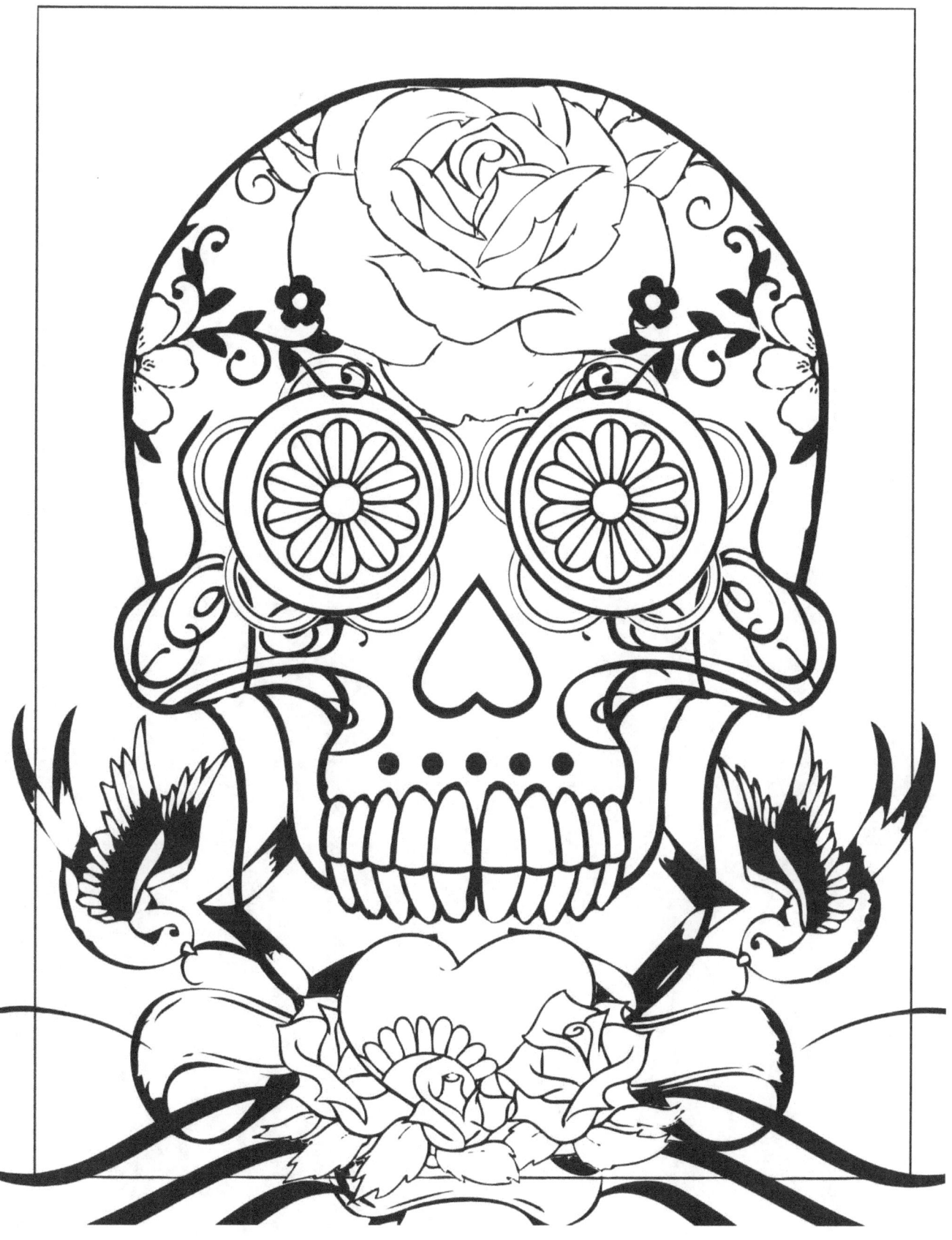

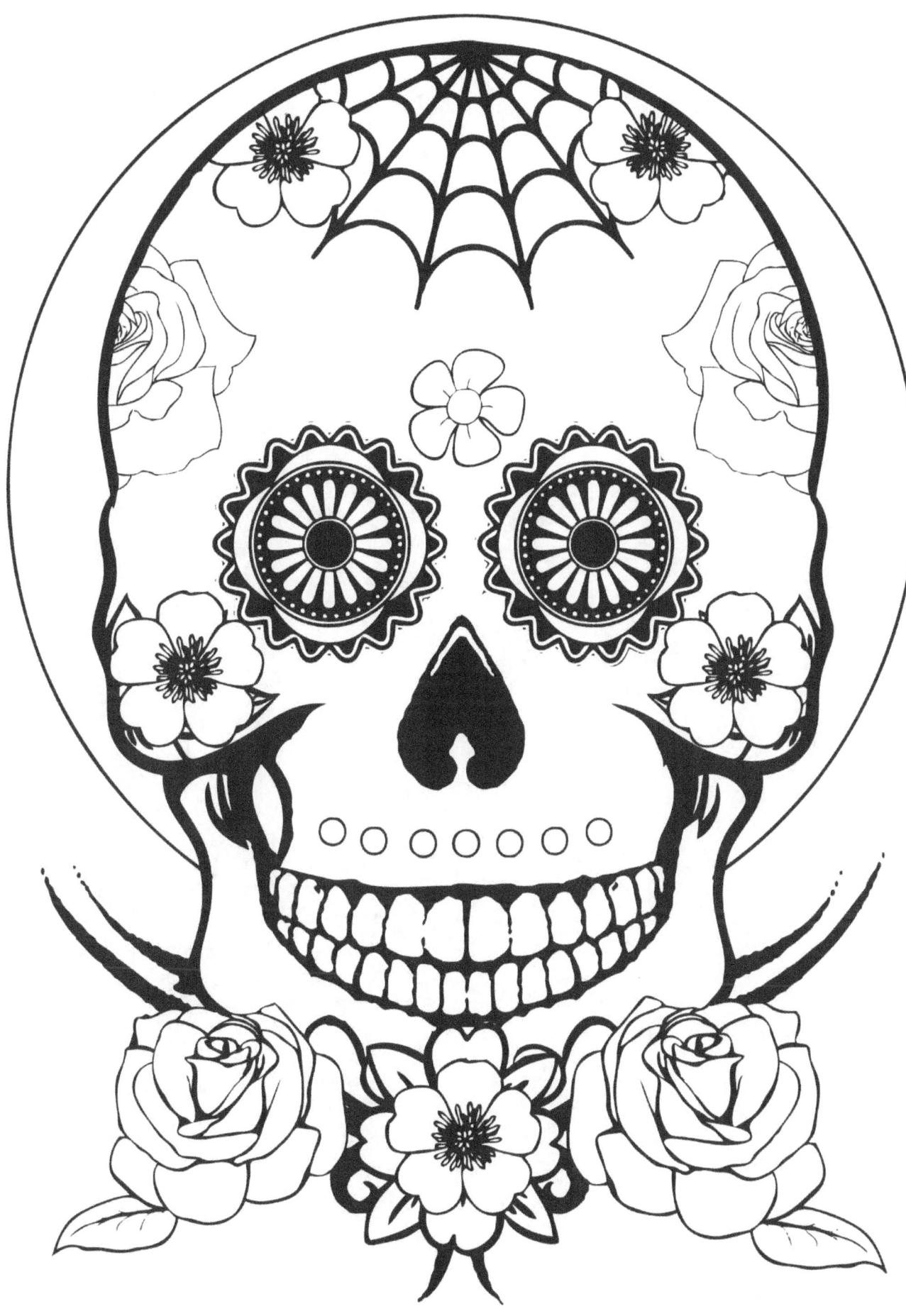

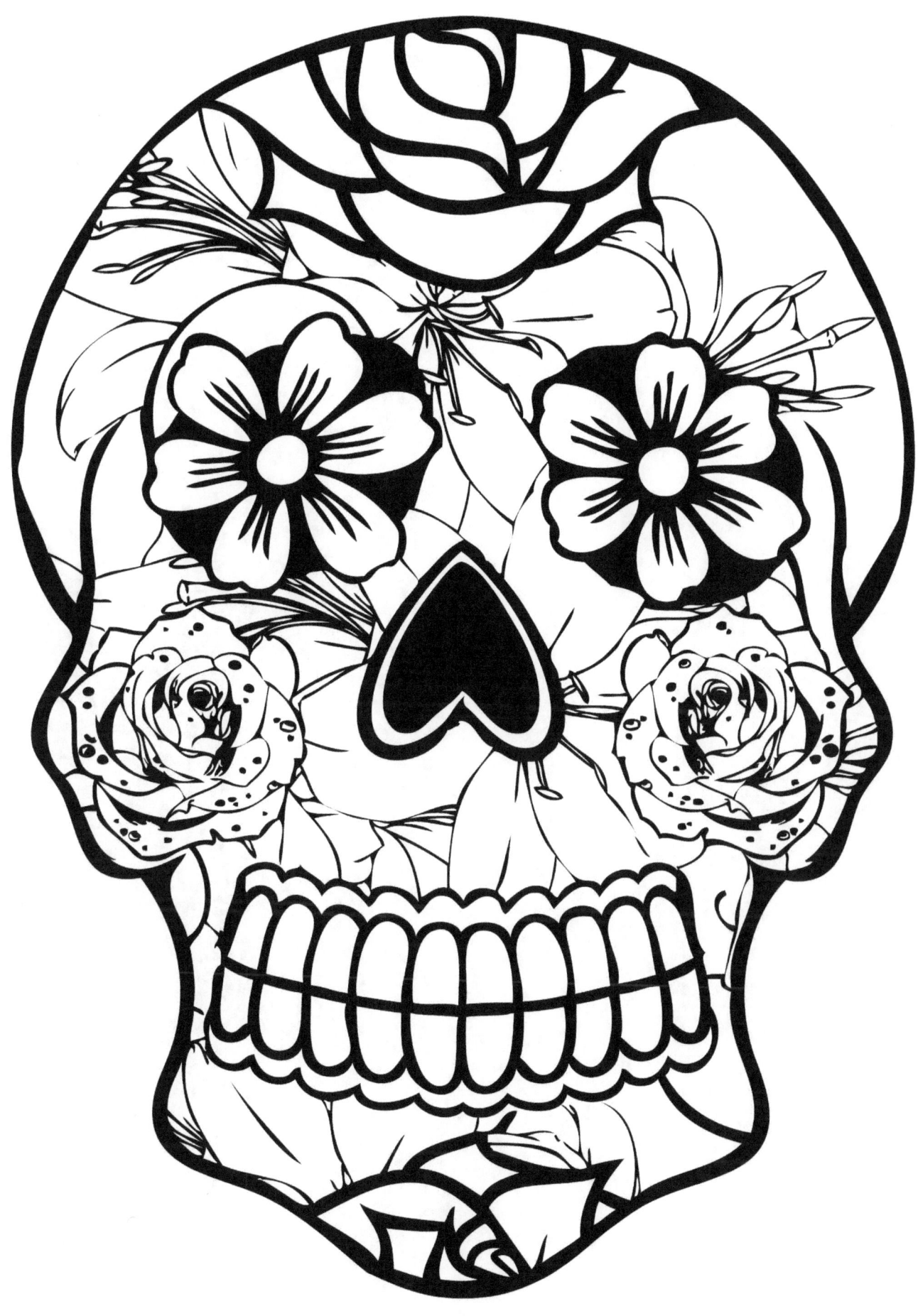

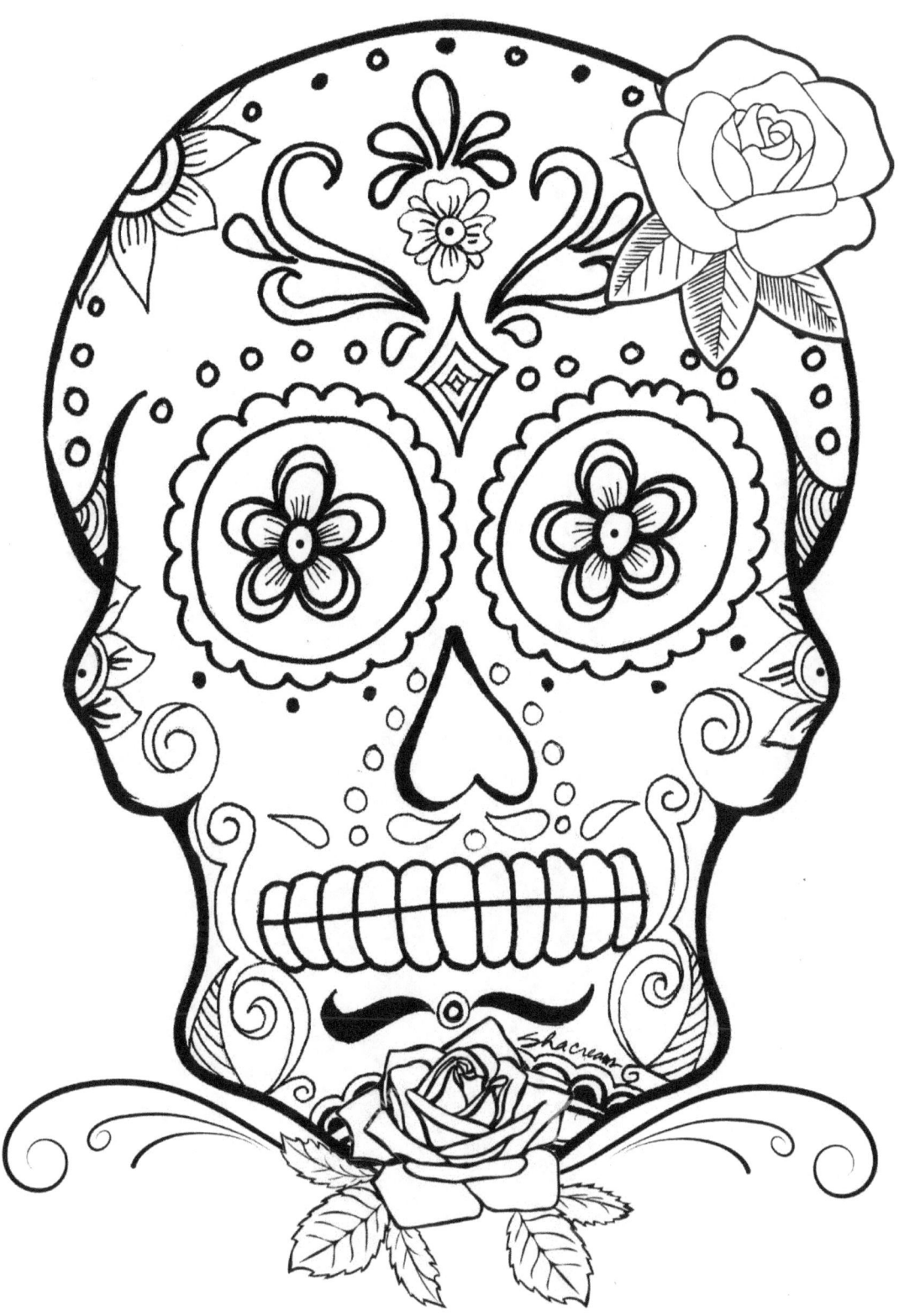

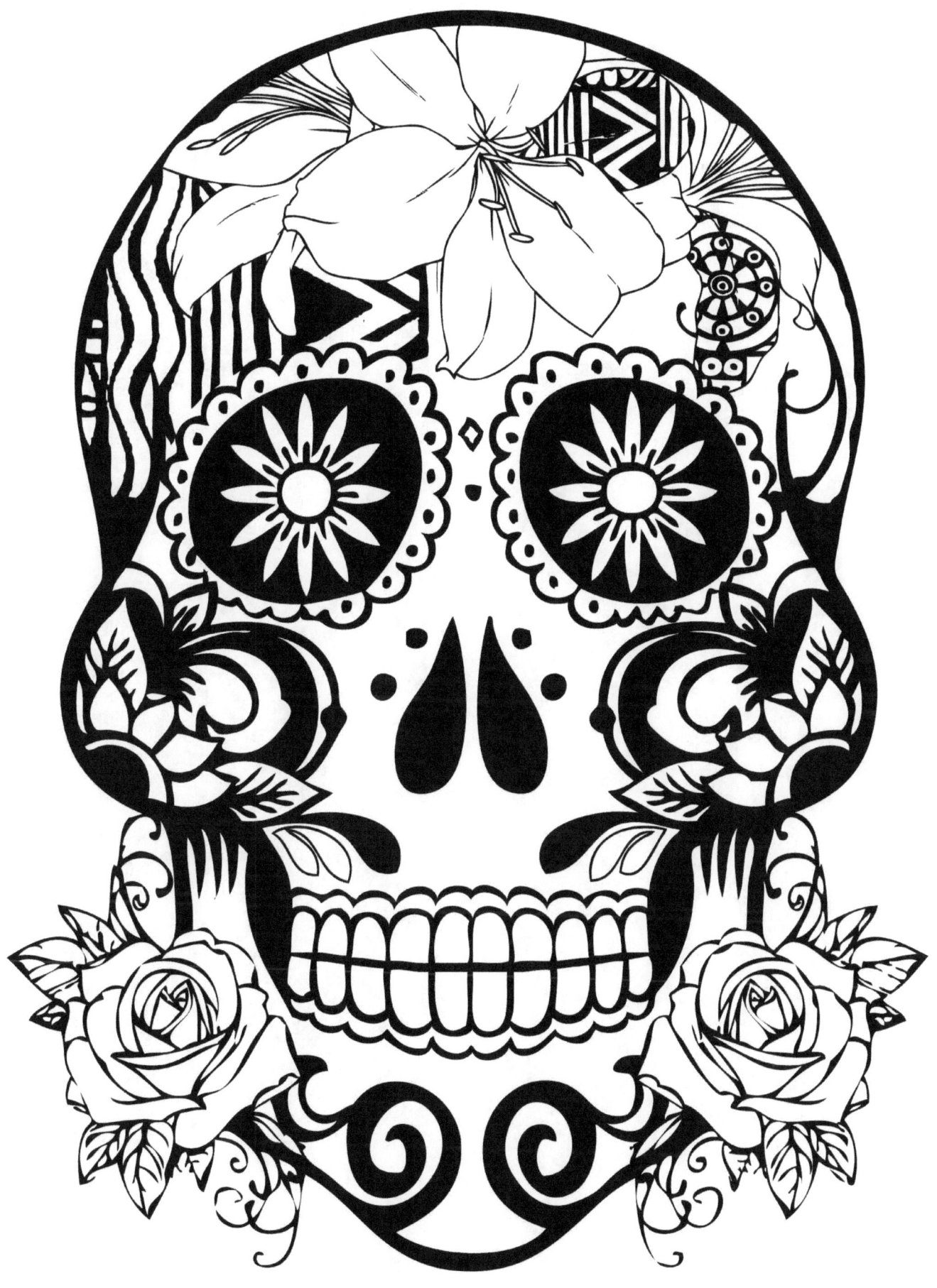

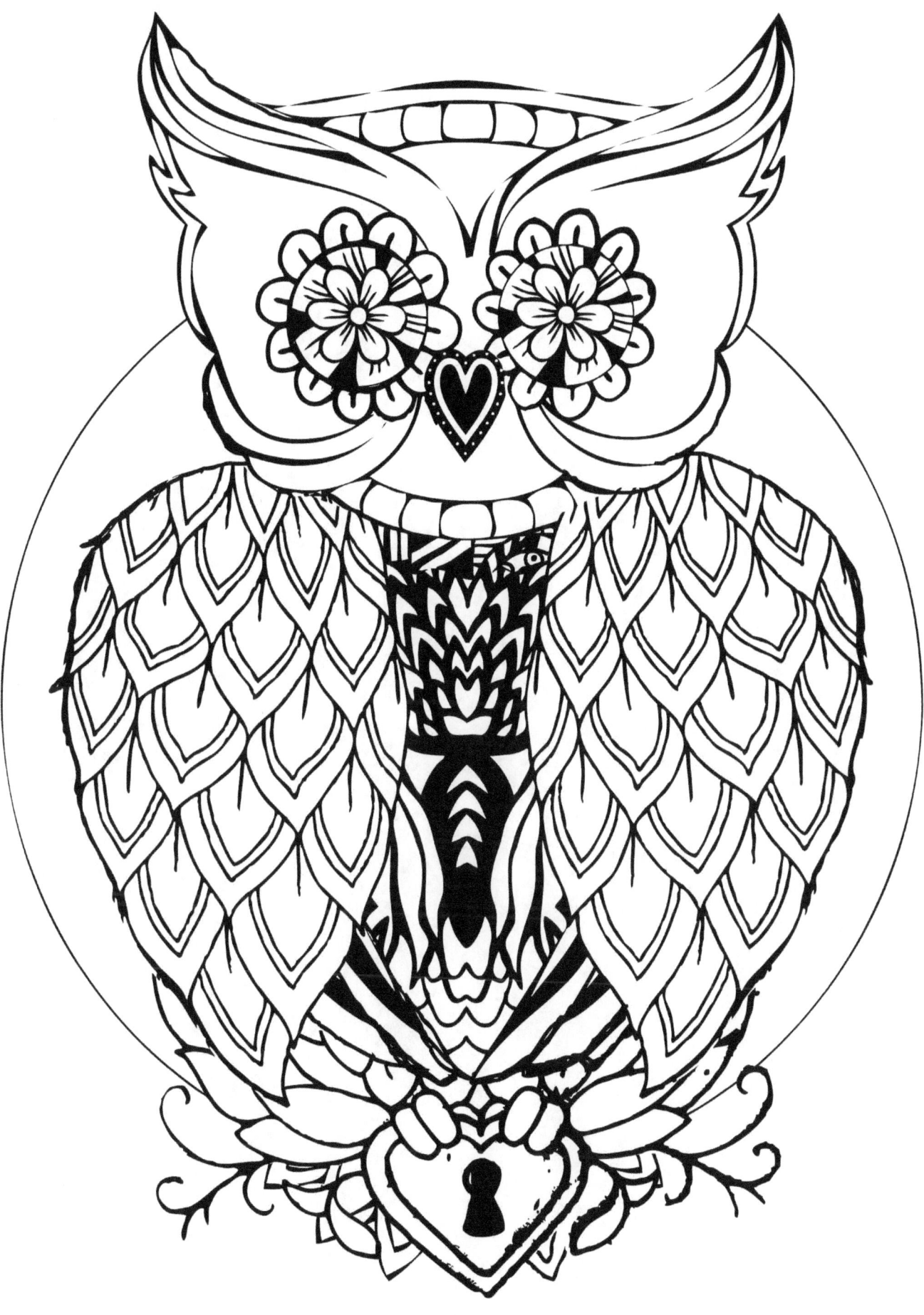

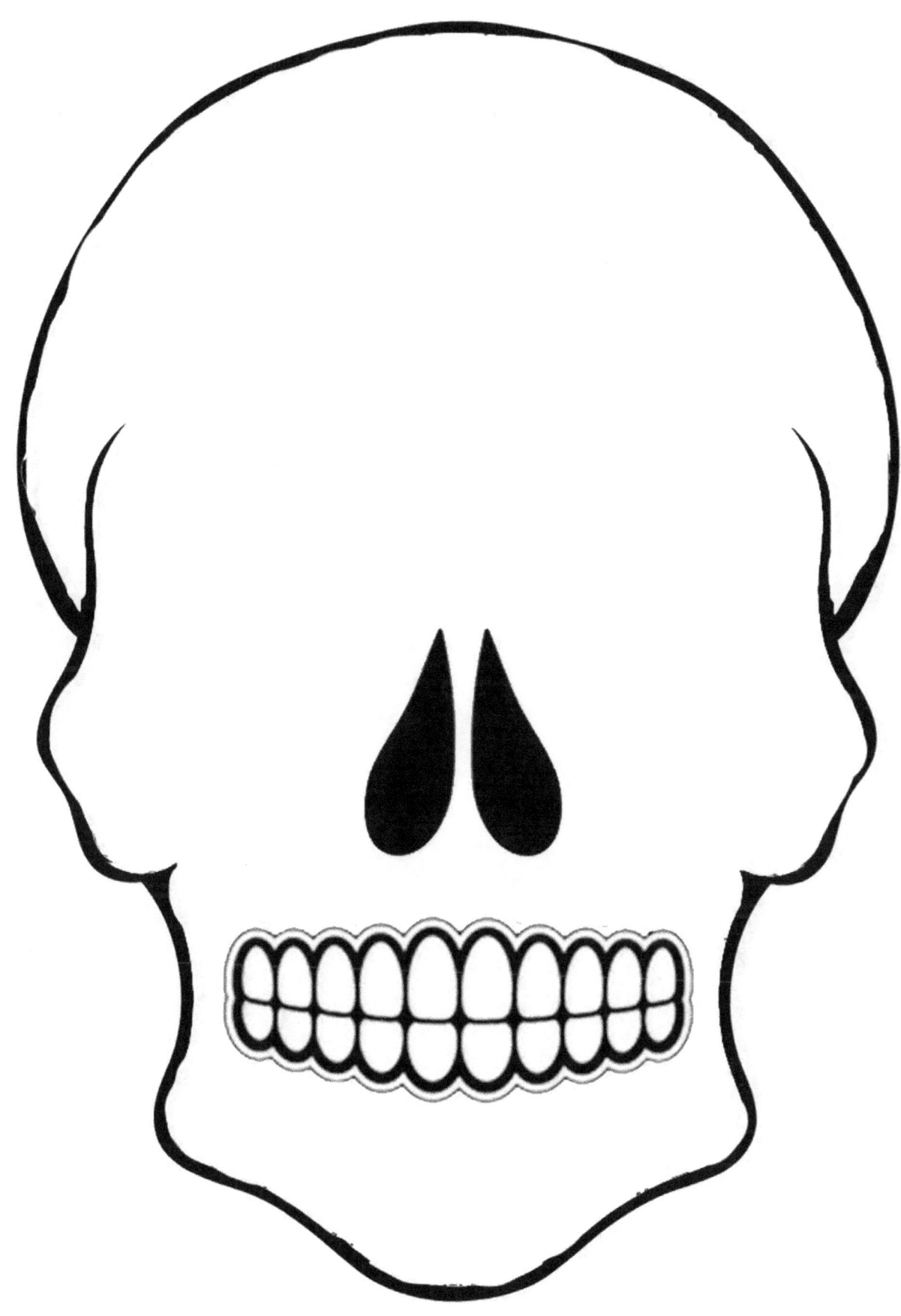

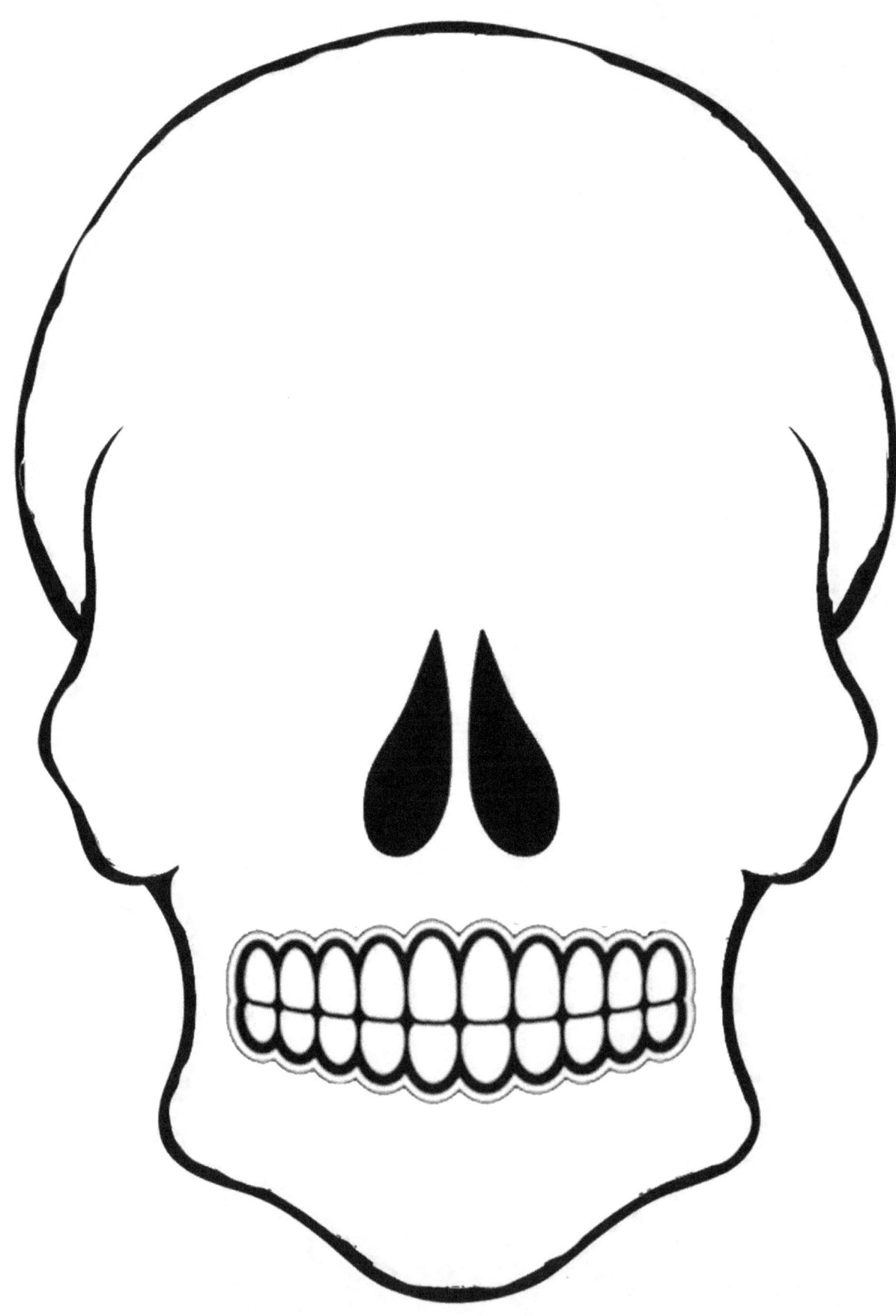

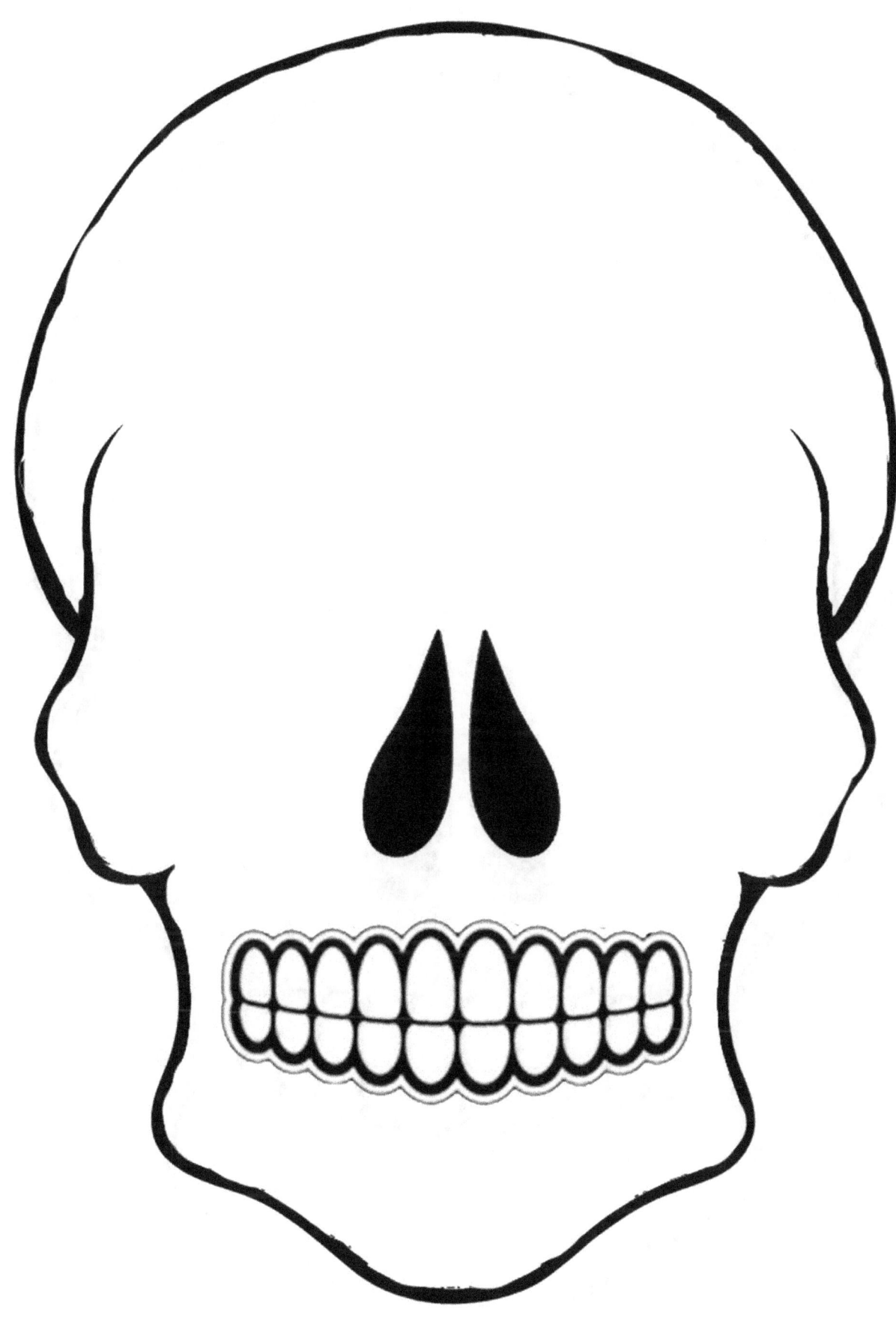

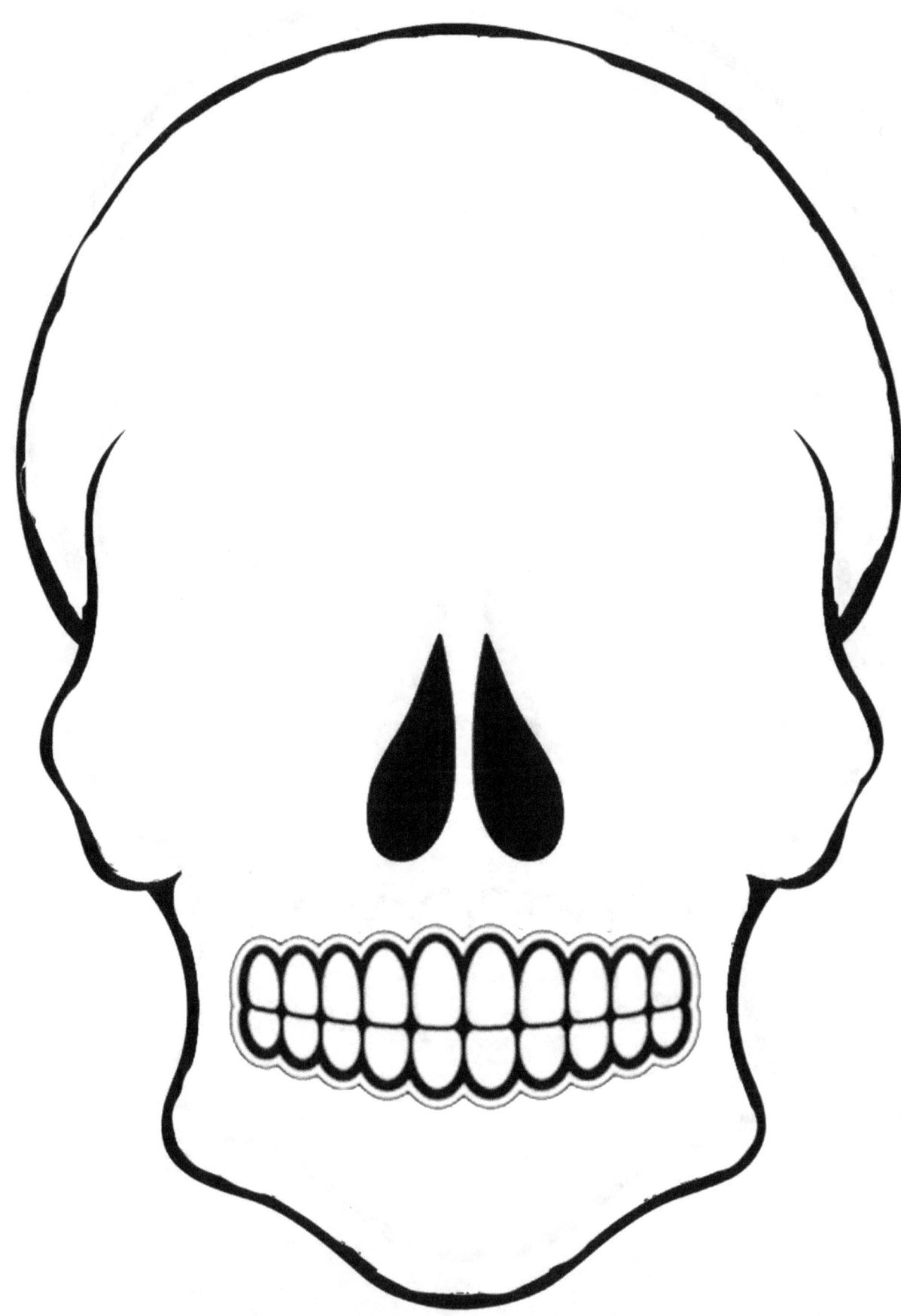

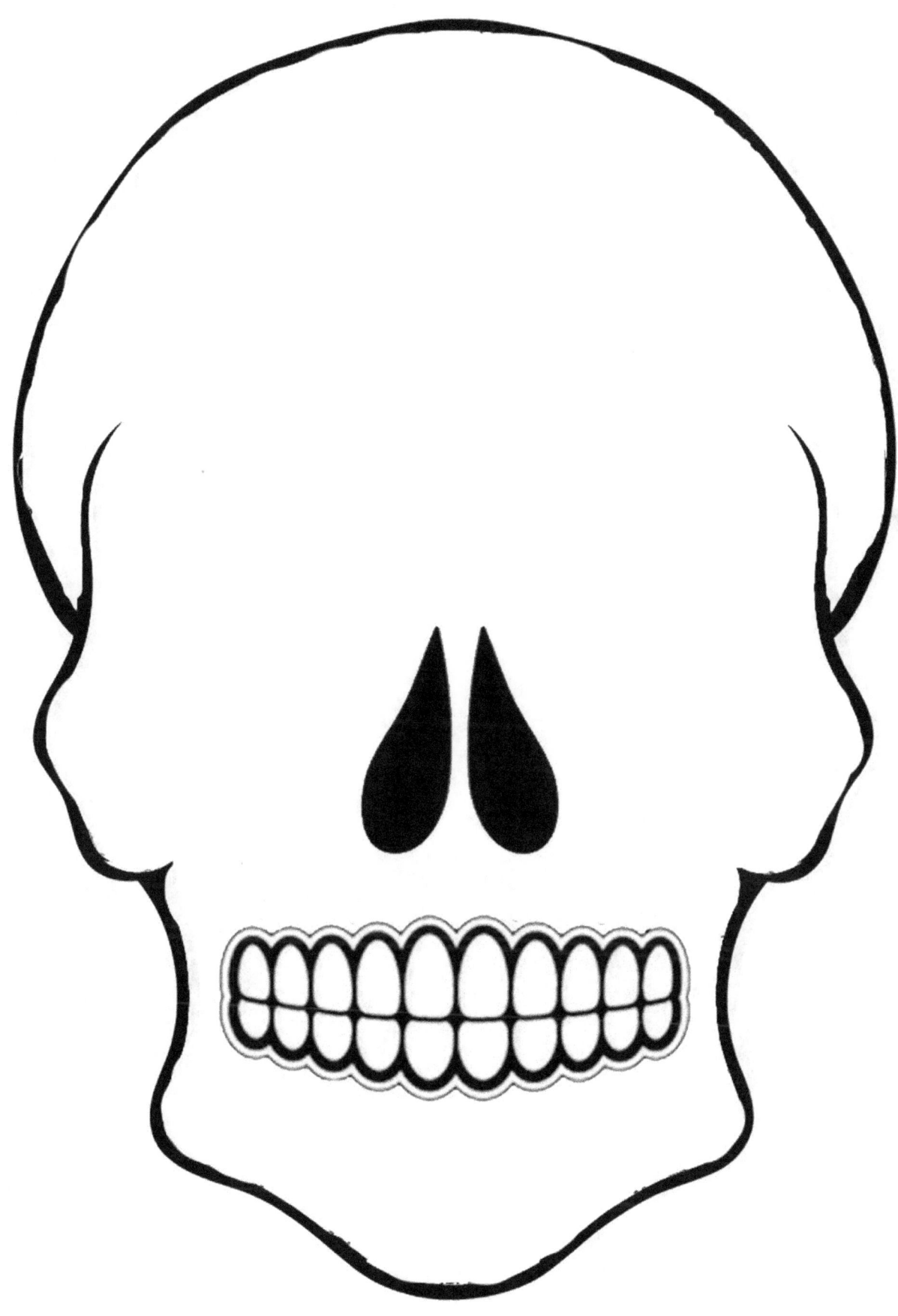

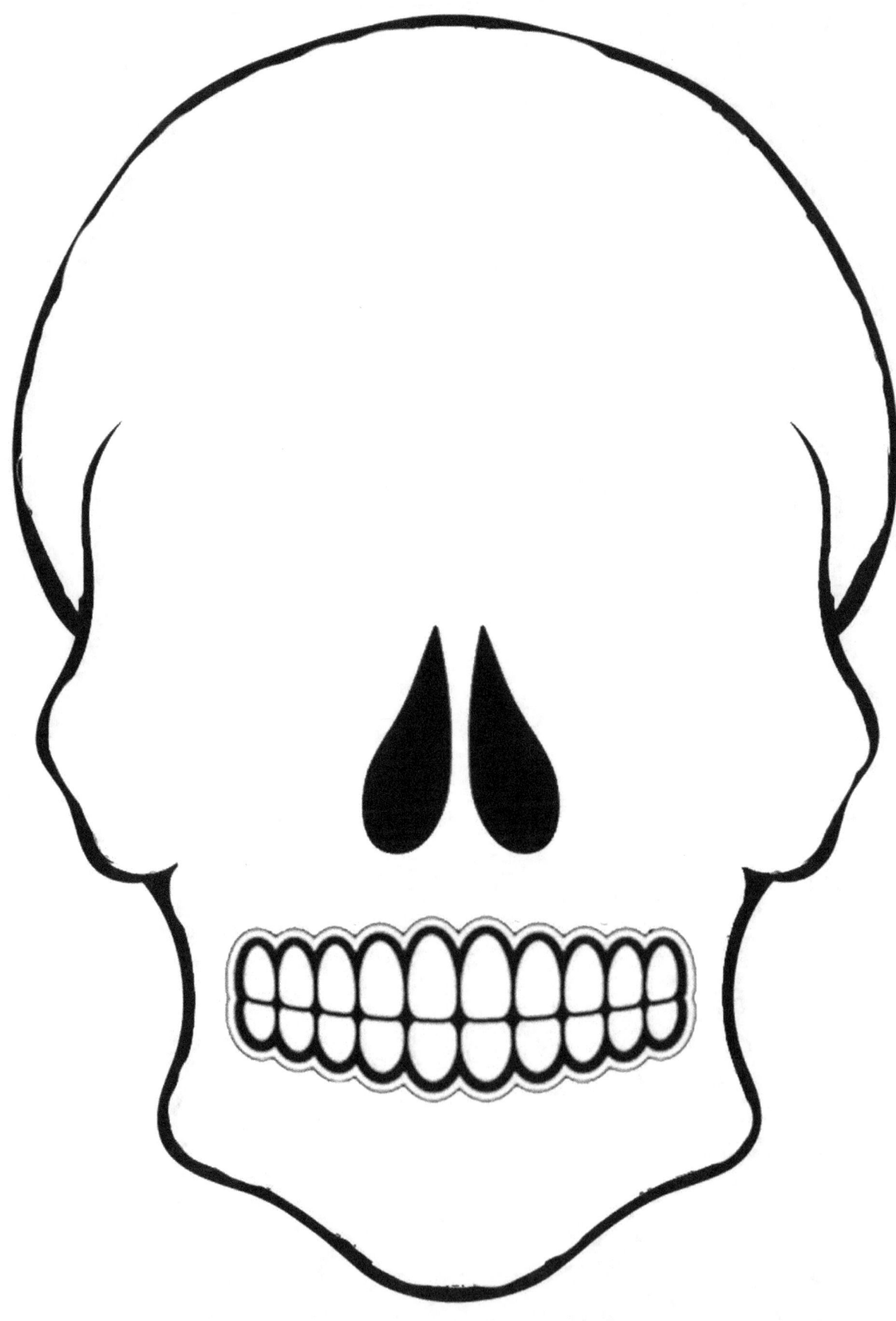

To See more of my work and to follow me

www.shacream.com

www.instragram.com/shacream.com

www.pintrest.com/shacream

www.ingramcontent.com/pod-product-compliance
Lightning Source LLC
Chambersburg PA
CBHW080537190526
45169CB00007B/2537